CONTENTS

AREA MAP SHOWING THE FIFE AND CENTRAL REGION
AIRFIELDS IN THE SECOND WORLD WAR

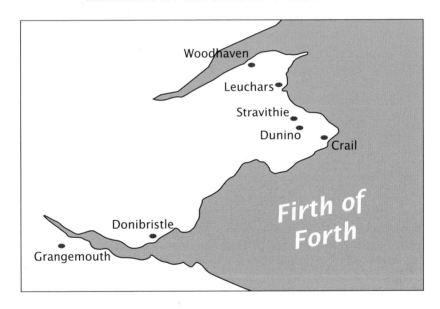

SCOTTISH AIRFIELDS IN THE SECOND WORLD WAR

VOL. 2
FIFE AND CENTRAL REGION

Martyn Chorlton

COUNTRYSIDE BOOKS
NEWBURY BERKSHIRE

First published 2009
© Martyn Chorlton 2009

COUNTRYSIDE BOOKS
3 Catherine Road
Newbury, Berkshire

To view our complete range of books,
please visit us at
www.countrysidebooks.co.uk

ISBN 978 1 84674 148 7

The cover picture from an original painting by Colin Doggett
shows Hudson 1 N7217 of 224 Squadron
shooting down the RAF's first official kill of the
Second World War, a Dornier Do18
flying boat in October 1939

Produced through MRM Associates Ltd., Reading
Typeset by CJWT Solutions, St Helens
Printed by Information Press, Oxford

*All material for the manufacture of this book
was sourced from sustainable forests*

I

SETTING
THE SCENE

First World War

Three of the airfields in Fife covered within this volume can trace their roots back to the First World War. Land near the village of Leuchars takes the honour of being the first of the three sites to have received military aircraft, when Royal Flying Corps (RFC) aircraft landed at St Andrews en route to Montrose in 1914. The land was later developed into the airfield that is still resident there today. In fact, aviation activity near the site can be traced back even further, the Royal Engineers having experimented with balloons there in 1911. Despite these early connections, however, the airfield was not ready for occupation until November 1918.

Donibristle was the first airfield to be established in the region, albeit under slightly false pretences. As part of the aerial defence of the Firth of Forth and Edinburgh, and as a direct result of attacks on Scotland's capital by Zeppelin airships, 77 (Home Defence) Squadron was formed. The main unit was established at Turnhouse, but it needed several emergency landing grounds which were to be dispersed around the region. Simultaneously, the Royal Naval Air Service (RNAS) were surveying airfield sites around the new Rosyth shipyard for the potential storage of large numbers of aircraft destined to serve with the Grand Fleet. It was, however, the RFC who were first to establish a small landing ground on land belonging to the Earl of Moray at Donibristle House. Much to the Earl's displeasure, trees were cleared and a guard hut and a few buildings were constructed, but 77 Squadron was destined never to use the fledgling airfield.

Taken over by the RNAS in August 1917, expansion and construction on the site was rapid. Hangars 200 ft long and 100 ft wide were built to store over 50 aircraft intended to operate with the Grand Fleet during the spring of 1918. The end of the First World War curtailed the use of these aircraft but the airfield at Donibristle continued to grow.

Crail, like Donibristle, was heavily developed during the final months of the First World War and like so many others was closed by late 1919. In contrast, Donibristle broke all the rules and because of its useful positioning near the Rosyth Naval Dockyard remained in use after the Armistice and beyond.

Between the Wars

Donibristle's workload during the 1920s far exceeded that of all the other airfields in the area. Its Fleet Aircraft Repair Depot was busy overhauling aircraft for service on carriers until 1921. There was then a temporary lull in activities until 1925 when a variety of flying units passed through the airfield up to the beginning of the Second World War. Donibristle became associated with torpedo-dropping trials and with RAF units that reformed as torpedo-bomber squadrons equipped with the Hawker Horsley (36 Squadron) and Vickers Vildebeest (22 and 42 Squadrons).

Hawker Horsleys of 36 (Torpedo Bomber) Squadron, at Donibristle during 1930. (via A. P. Ferguson)

Leuchars received the first of its many units on 1st March 1920, when 203 Squadron was reformed with Sopwith Camels, but units associated with the Fleet Air Arm (FAA) were more common than RAF squadrons all the way through the 1920s and up to the mid-1930s. A change of role came in 1935 when 1 Flying Training School (FTS) was reformed at Leuchars on 1st April. The school, with a huge cross-section of aircraft at its disposal, was mainly responsible for the training of FAA officers. By August 1938, 1 FTS had moved south to Netheravon in Wiltshire and for the first time in its history, RAF Leuchars came under the total control of the RAF, namely Coastal Command. It would remain in this role until 1950.

A new civilian airfield – and a great hope as the Central Scotland Airport – was built at Grangemouth. After many years and much heartache the new and impressive municipal airport was opened, with pomp and ceremony, on 1st May 1939. Everyone was well aware that another conflict was drawing closer and sadly, like so many small airports during the late 1930s, Grangemouth's civilian operations were halted by the beginning of the Second World War.

Flying boat and seaplane operations from the River Tay first began across the water at Dundee in 1918. A new flying boat station was established at Woodhaven in 1938, initially serving the needs of Short Sunderland units. Activity was limited but steadily increased during 1939 and the base would continue to serve for the next six years.

Second World War

When Great Britain declared war on Germany on 3rd September 1939, very few of Scotland's airfields were ready for action. Thankfully though, Fife was lucky enough to have at least one airfield that was active and fully prepared. Leuchars, with its two Lockheed Hudson squadrons at readiness, was involved in the conflict from its beginning through to its end in Europe in May 1945. Aircraft from the airfield had in fact been carrying out coastal and shipping patrols for several months before war was declared.

As the war progressed, more airfields would be built, while those that were already established changed their roles throughout the duration of the conflict.

Fighter Squadrons

The number of RAF fighter squadrons operating out of Fife during the Second World War could be counted on one hand. While fighter defence was important, the main defending units were located south of the Firth of Forth and north of the Tay. Leuchars supported two fighter detachments during November 1940: firstly, 65 Squadron from Turnhouse in Midlothian with Hawker Hurricane Is; secondly, 72 Squadron from Coltishall in Norfolk with Supermarine Spitfire Is. Both detachments lasted for just three weeks, and very little detail was recorded about their time at Leuchars.

Keeping with the tradition of naming their airfields after birds, Crail was commissioned as HMS Jackdaw on 1st October 1940.

Crail also briefly hosted an RAF fighter squadron, when 43 Squadron with Hurricane Is arrived from Drem in February 1941. Scrambled on many occasions during their stay, the RAF way of doing things was often frowned upon by their Royal Navy hosts.

Grangemouth, despite the fact that its location made it susceptible to poor weather, was initially home to several fighter units which were being shuffled around the region. An Auxiliary Air Force unit, 602 (City of Glasgow) Squadron, passed through in October 1939 and was followed by at least two detachments from 141 Squadron. This pioneering night-fighter unit was equipped with the Boulton Paul Defiant but never found any prey whilst operating over the Firth of Forth. The Hurricanes of 263 Squadron were often scrambled from Grangemouth despite the squadron going through the protracted process of re-equipping with the twin-engined Westland Whirlwind I. The Hurricanes were only meant to be used by 263 Squadron as a temporary measure, but their service was extended as it took many months for the unit to become fully operational on the troublesome Whirlwind fighter.

The FAA also brought a wide variety of fighter aircraft into the region, some of which equipped operational squadrons while others

Aircrew of 309 Squadron at Dunino in 1941.

were used for training. The first unit to arrive at Crail, on 8th October 1940, was 800 Squadron, equipped with the Blackburn Roc I two-seat carrier-based fighter. The unit only stayed for a few days, but many more would follow. FAA fighter types such as the Fairey Fulmar, Grumman Martlet and Wildcat, Supermarine Seafire, Hawker Hurricane, Chance Vought Corsair and Grumman Hellcat, to name but a few, were all seen at Crail, Donibristle and, to a lesser extent at Dunino, throughout the Second World War.

The Fleet Air Arm

Countless FAA units passed through Fife during the Second World War. Donibristle, commissioned as HMS *Merlin*, received several squadrons per month as well as the constant stream of naval aircraft passing through the repair yard. Work began on Fife's second big naval airfield only two days before the start of the war. Crail, commissioned as HMS *Jackdaw*, was ready to receive its first unit on 1st October 1940 and quickly established itself as the Admiralty's premier torpedo training station. Resident training squadrons were formed, two of which remained at the airfield throughout the war. As was the case at Donibristle, operational squadrons came and went, often staying for only a few days. Just as many again were formed or reformed at the naval airfields.

To relieve the pressure, a third naval airfield was commissioned at Dunino, not far from Crail. First recognised as a satellite to Crail in October 1940, the airfield was initially used by several RAF squadrons before being commissioned as HMS *Jackdaw II* in December 1942. Not the best of sites for an airfield, Dunino still managed to house many FAA squadrons. By the end of the war, however, it was relegated to the mass storage of Fairey Barracudas before being closed to flying in 1946.

Coastal Command

Leuchars came under the control of 18 Group, RAF Coastal Command, from 1938 through to 1950, the airfield's position lending itself perfectly to operations over the North Sea and the Norwegian and Danish coasts. Hudson-equipped squadrons carried the fight across the sea during the early days of the Second World War, the aircraft being used to attack shipping, port facilities and airfields. Spending hours navigating across open seas took great skill and determination. Always in the back of each crewmember's mind was the knowledge that their chances of rescue should they have to ditch at sea were remote.

Beaufort and Hampden torpedo squadrons followed and, with the arrival of the Bristol Beaufighter, more and more enemy trawlers were sent to the bottom of the sea. The de Havilland Mosquito joined the Beaufighters in 1943, not only providing long-range fighter protection but also the capability to attack shipping targets. This combination of aircraft proved to be a potent coastal strike team, claiming thousands of tons of shipping sunk before the war's end.

Consolidated Catalina operations by 333 Squadron at Woodhaven were also under the control of Leuchars and Coastal Command. This small but valuable Norwegian-manned unit discreetly traversed the North Sea carrying out many covert operations in support of their fellow countrymen.

From July 1944 onwards, the first of two long-range Consolidated Liberator squadrons arrived at Leuchars. The Liberator operated from Leuchars mainly in the anti-submarine role, using the powerful Leigh Light to catch U-boats on the surface. More Liberator units followed and it was with this type that Leuchars entered post-war

A Bristol Beaufort I of 42 Squadron between sorties at Leuchars in early 1941.

peace only to encounter a new kind of conflict a few years later: the Cold War.

Training

Many airfields, at one stage or another during the Second World War, hosted a training unit and this part of Scotland was no exception, with long-term residents such as 58 Operational Training Unit (OTU) at Grangemouth worthy of mention. This particular OTU spent its entire existence at Grangemouth, specifically to train fighter pilots to fly and fight in the Supermarine Spitfire. Student pilots from all over the world came to Grangemouth and, while many went on to fly and fight with front-line squadrons, a large number never made it through their training. The loss rate was incredibly high, but this was sadly typical of all such OTUs.

Crail was home to many training squadrons throughout the Second World War. Being a specialist torpedo training unit, HMS *Jackdaw* had two resident units, namely 785 and 786 Squadrons, the former serving at the airfield from 1941 to 1946. The very nature of torpedo training resulted in many accidents and because the training was conducted over water, the odds of surviving an accident were dramatically cut.

11

Second World War Remnants Today

Out of the seven aviation sites covered in this book, only one is still active and of the remainder, all but one still have sufficient remains and remnants to connect them with an aviation past. The exception is Woodhaven, although it could be argued that the runway is still intact!

Crail leads as probably one of the best-preserved disused airfields in Scotland, if not Great Britain. With over 150 buildings still remaining, plus its runways and impressive control tower, it is a great example of an FAA airfield. Standing in the middle of this exposed airfield and looking back towards the empty control tower certainly sends a shiver down the spine. With very little effort, it is easy to imagine the airfield in its heyday with Swordfish and Barracudas coming and going. Donibristle, by contrast, has succumbed to industrial and housing development. However, many military buildings still remain, incorporated into the industrial infrastructure, including several dating back to the 1920s.

The Swordfish was a common sight at Crail throughout the Second World War. This one, like so many others, is performing seemingly endless circuits and bumps.

Dunino is located in beautiful countryside and is easily missed by those with no interest in such sites. From a ground personnel point of view it would have been a lovely posting but from a pilot's viewpoint, Dunino was a particularly challenging airfield to operate from. Many buildings survive, tucked away amongst the trees, while the unusual control tower still stands on the edge of the airfield. The old flying field, long since returned to agriculture, is intact and the skeletal remains of several hangars add to the atmosphere.

Like Donibristle, the usual physical signs of an airfield have long since been removed at Grangemouth. However, the two large aircraft hangars still remain, although the central terminal area is long gone, the frontage and control tower having succumbed to a fire in 1952. The old technical area is now known as the Abbotsinch Industrial Estate and a small memorial cairn was erected at the entrance in 1994 to commemorate the many pilots who lost their lives whilst undergoing training at 58 OTU. The airfield itself has been taken over by housing and the expansion of the nearby oil terminal.

It could be suggested that the ex-Satellite Landing Ground at Stravithie is virtually complete. The airfield probably looks no different from the day when it was abandoned during the closing months of the Second World War.

The Panavia Tornado F.3s operated by 43(F) Squadron and here with 111(F) Squadron are the current defenders of the United Kingdom's northern airspace.

13

As old as the RAF itself, Leuchars is still owned and operated by the Ministry of Defence and remains one of the most active RAF stations in Great Britain. Used continuously since its opening in 1918, Leuchars is one of the few military airfields with First World War buildings still in use. Four Belfast Truss hangars still survive, making the plethora of Second World War buildings seem almost inconsequential. While the main runway has been extended to nearly 8,500 ft in length, both runways are in the same positions as those of the originals laid during the war. Now supporting two Panavia Tornado F.3 air defence squadrons, Leuchars' geographical position means that the airfield's future should be assured for many years to come.

2
CRAIL

The remote but beautiful fishing village of Crail, located at Fife's most easterly point, lent its name to two airfields during the 20th century. The first briefly opened during the latter stages of the First World War, only to be reopened during the early months of the Second World War. Supporting at least 36 Fleet Air Arm (FAA) squadrons alone during the Second World War, Crail became the premier and most important airfield for training aircrews in the art of attacking the enemy using a torpedo.

Opened in July 1918, Crail's first airfield was a well-equipped and complex site with no less that seven Belfast Truss hangars plus a host of technical and domestic buildings. The flying field took up approximately 170 acres of land making it sufficient in size to cater for all of the aircraft of the day. Construction of the airfield was originally commissioned for use by the Royal Flying Corps (RFC) and Royal Naval Air Service (RNAS) but by the time it opened, the RAF had been formed and thus took control of the new airfield. The first unit to arrive was 58 Training (ex-Reserve) Squadron from Spittlegate in Lincolnshire on 15th July 1918, followed by 64 Training (ex-Reserve) Squadron from Harlaxton, also in Lincolnshire. Both squadrons brought a variety of aircraft with them including examples of the Armstrong Whitworth FK3, Nieuport 17, Royal Aircraft Factory FE2b, Maurice Farman Shorthorn, Avro 504 and many more. Both of these units were subsequently disbanded into 27 Training Depot Station (TDS), which was formed at Crail on 15th August 1918 and controlled by 20 Group, whose headquarters were at 14 Randolph Crescent, Edinburgh. In May 1918, 20 Group was renamed the North Western Area and assumed the responsibility of controlling all of Scotland's TDSs.

In addition to the RFC units based at Crail during the latter stages of

SCOTTISH AIRFIELDS IN THE SECOND WORLD WAR – VOL. 2 FIFE AND CENTRAL REGION

the First World War, a detachment of the 120th Aero Squadron, United States Army Air Corps made use of the airfield during August 1918 while they trained to fly the Avro 504 and Sopwith Pup.

With the end of the First World War, the RAF was wound down dramatically. Among the many units to be axed was 27 TDS, which disbanded on 31st March 1919. This left Crail with only a Delivery Station (Storage), which had formed on 1st March 1919, and 104 Squadron, which had arrived at Crail on 3rd March as a cadre, having disposed of its de Havilland DH9s and DH10s. The squadron's personnel remained at Crail until the unit was disbanded on 30th June 1919. This marked the end for Crail which, despite so much money, time and effort having been invested to build this significant aerodrome, was closed in late 1919. By the early 1920s, the flying field had returned to the plough and the substantial hangars and buildings were all demolished not long thereafter.

The rebirth of Crail airfield came about as a direct result of Donibristle's lack of and need for a Relief Landing Ground (RLG). Unlike Crail, Donibristle managed to survive the widespread and radical closures of RAF facilities in the immediate aftermath of the First World War, thus maintaining an all-important foothold for the Royal Navy in Scotland. The old landing ground at Crail was surveyed, as were two other potential sites, but it was obvious that the former was the most suitable of the three. Over 550 acres of land were purchased from local farmers for the construction of what was planned to be a considerably larger airfield than had been built on the site twenty years earlier. Construction work began on 1st September 1939 and continued for over a year before the new airfield was completed. This timescale is not surprising though, for the finished airfield had nearly 200 brick buildings, four runways, and a three-storey control tower capable of surviving a direct hit from an enemy bomb.

A four-runway configuration was standard for all of the Royal Navy's airfields at the time. Although three runways were usually sufficient on a typical RAF station, the Royal Navy would always design their airfields with an aircraft carrier mentality. Hence a runway, like a carrier, would always be positioned into wind, which in Crail's case was usually regular and often severe. The main runway measured 1,200 yds in length and the other three were each 1,000 yds – all more than adequate for FAA aircraft of the period. By way of comparison, the average length of the flying deck of an aircraft carrier at the time was approximately 250 yds! Most of the Royal Navy's airfields also had a three-storey control tower to replicate the conning tower of an aircraft carrier. The tower at Crail was of this design and was particularly substantial in the event of an enemy attack. It is possible that it was also beefed up to cope with the weather, given its exposed position facing out to the Firth of Forth.

Eight 60 x 70 ft hangars were built, four for storage and four for aircraft. In addition, a single 185 x 110 ft Aircraft Repair Shed hangar and eight Superblisters were dispersed around the edge of the airfield. Accommodation was described as 'temporary' but several seaside hotels were requisitioned for service personnel.

Only days after construction work commenced, a new Wireless Experimental Unit (WEU) was opened up at Crail on 29th October 1939. They may only have needed a wooden hut to operate from and initially they were accommodated at Leuchars. Their work was secret enough for the officers and fourteen other ranks that worked there to warrant their own military guard at Leuchars. It is quite possible that the WEU personnel were the embryo for the Kingsbarns wireless station, which would have a direct connection to telegraphists based at Crail.

Before construction of the airfield was completed, one of many air raids on the Firth of Forth came very close to Crail. During an attack on a convoy in the Firth on 18th July 1940, the Luftwaffe also took the opportunity to bomb the Anstruther Radio Direction Finder Station and Crail village. No damage was caused to the airfield and construction work continued unabated. The Luftwaffe returned to Crail on 18th October when a Junkers Ju 88 dropped five High Explosive (HE) and two oil bombs near the village. A searchlight post, west of the village, was attacked with machine-gun fire during the same raid.

There was no anti-aircraft protection for the airfield during the early stages of the war, all of the main batteries being located around Edinburgh and Rosyth Naval Dockyard. Crail did at least have a decoy airfield located at Boghall, north of Kingsbarns, approximately three miles north of Crail. Illuminated brightly at night to mimic Crail, no attacks were ever recorded there but it may have deterred the odd one. By the winter of 1941, Crail did at least have a detachment of twelve men from the Royal Artillery manning a single 40mm Vickers machine gun. A twin Bofors anti-aircraft gun was also established above Kingsbarns, but its main use proved to be as a practice target for Blackburn Skuas used to train FAA crews in the art of dive-bombing.

Crail was officially opened on 1st October 1940, as Royal Naval Air Station (RNAS) HMS *Jackdaw* under the command of Capt F. M.

Walton. The main role of the airfield during the Second World War was the training of Torpedo Bomber Reconnaissance (TBR) aircrews for service with the FAA. However, before a resident unit was formed to carry out such training, the honour of being the first flying squadron to pass through Crail went to an FAA fighter unit, 800 Squadron, under the command of Lt R. M. Smeeton. The squadron, equipped with Blackburn Roc Is, arrived at Crail on 8th October 1940 from HMS *Ark Royal*. Three weeks later, the unit left for Prestwick in Ayrshire and returned to their carrier a few days later.

The Roc fighters were followed at Crail by Fairey Albacore I torpedo bombers, the first to arrive being those of 827 Squadron from Yeovilton in Somerset on 2nd November, followed the next day by 829 Squadron from St Eval in Cornwall. The latter unit only stayed for a couple of weeks, while 827 Squadron eventually departed to the carrier HMS *Argus* for Deck Landing Training (DLT) on 14th March 1941.

On 4th November 1940, the first of two dedicated TBR training squadrons was formed at Crail. Commanded by Lt Cdr P. G. O. Sydney-Turner, 785 Squadron was initially equipped with thirteen Blackburn Shark IIs and five Fairey Swordfish Is, but within a few months the Shark II was deemed obsolete for TBR training and was

With the Isle of May in the distance and an Albacore following behind, a Swordfish of 785 Squadron prepares to drop its 'dummy' torpedo.

Fairey Albacores of 785 and 786 Squadrons are prepared for another practice torpedo drop in the Firth of Forth. (via R. C. Sturtivant)

replaced by the Albacore I in August 1941. The Albacore had itself been introduced into FAA service to replace the Fairey Swordfish. However, the superb Swordfish, affectionately known as the 'Stringbag', would continue to serve the FAA throughout the Second World War and achieve more successes against the enemy than the Albacore.

The second of Crail's TBR training units was 786 Squadron, which was formed at the base on 21st November 1940. Under the command of Capt F. W. Brown, the unit was first equipped with nine Albacore Is and was specifically formed to operate alongside 785 Squadron. It was increased in size from mid-1941 when it began to receive Swordfish Is and the rare, American-built Vought-Sikorsky Chesapeake I dive-bomber.

All pilots who passed through Crail during the Second World War would have been specifically selected for TBR training at an early stage in their military flying careers. Initially, they were taught to fly at very low levels over the sea whilst carrying a dummy torpedo. Although this sounds quite straightforward, travelling at high speed at 200 ft above the waves took a great deal of concentration and many trainee aircrews were lost in the process. The next stage of their training consisted of practice attacks on the many target ships which were at

Crail's disposal, either anchored or moving in the Firth of Forth. The vast majority of these ships were retired paddle steamers, cross-channel ferries and several obsolete Royal Navy ships. All were too large to berth at Crail village so they operated from Methil docks on the edge of Largo Bay.

Once the trainee aircrews were deemed proficient at approaching the target ship safely, they graduated to actually dropping a dummy torpedo. The dummies were in short supply during the early years of the war and so the next stage of training – dropping a 'runner' – was reached as quickly as possible. A 'runner' was exactly the same as a real torpedo but without a warhead. It was set to run deeper than a live example and once it had run its course, would rise to the surface for recovery and thus be available to be used again. Each torpedo was set to run deep so that it would pass beneath the target ship. If a 'runner' was to strike a ship's hull, there was a good chance that it would receive more damage than it would inflict on the ship itself.

During early 1941, Crail played host to a detachment of 812 Squadron operating Swordfish Is and a few days later, on 23rd January, a handful of Albacore Is from 828 Squadron. Flying training was severely hampered at the time by heavy snowfalls, but Crail's tarmac runways were relatively easy to keep clear. Airfields such as Drem, however, with grass runways, were struggling to operate so, on 22nd February, the Hurricane Is of 43 Squadron moved to Crail. The Royal Navy were used to running things their way at Crail and the activities of an RAF operational fighter squadron were alien to them. During 43 Squadron's first scramble from Crail, the RAF pilots sent the resident ratings flying and then took off without permission, crosswind and in tight formation. Senior Naval staff at Crail were unimpressed and ordered that the RAF should cease such dangerous flying immediately.

By 1st March, the weather had improved sufficiently to enable the Hurricanes of 43 Squadron to make the short flight back to their home airfield across the Forth, thus bringing to an end the one and only time that Crail would support an RAF fighter squadron. Other RAF aircraft did however use the base, most notably in its role as a useful emergency landing ground for all. One such was a Bristol Blenheim IV from 107 Squadron based at Leuchars, which found sanctuary at Crail when it crash-landed with engine trouble whilst outbound for convoy escort duty on 18th March 1941. None of the crew of the twin-engined aircraft was hurt in the incident.

A new Albacore unit, 831 Squadron, was formed at Crail on 1st

Albacores of 820 Squadron operating from Crail during late 1941. They would return with the Fairey Barracuda in 1944. (via R. C. Sturtivant)

April 1941. Under the command of Lt Cdr P. L. Mortimer and equipped with twelve Albacore Is, it was created as a torpedo spotter reconnaissance squadron which, after working up at Crail, moved to Machrihanish in Argyll on 26th August for a period of weapons training before embarking in the carrier HMS *Indomitable* in October.

Another long-term resident at Crail flew in from Donibristle on 1st June 1941. This was 770 Squadron, a Fleet Requirements Unit (FRU), which arrived with four Blackburn Roc Is under the command of Lt H. E. R. Torin. Two of these aircraft were employed as target tugs, the others were used for target-marking. Blackburn Skua IIs swelled the unit from October followed by a couple of Percival Proctor IIs before the year's end.

Throughout the remainder of 1941, two Albacore units (820 and 828 Squadrons) plus two Swordfish units (819 and 823 Squadrons) were each resident for a few weeks at a time at Crail. The last of this quartet of units was reformed at Crail on 1st November 1941 as a TBR unit equipped with nine Swordfish Is. Before working up, the squadron moved to Fraserburgh on 6th December. The other Swordfish-equipped unit, 819 Squadron, which arrived from Lee-on-Solent in Hampshire on 10th December, remained at Crail slightly longer. Training began almost immediately with the focus on torpedo-dropping and night-flying. Poor weather in January 1942 almost wiped out the squadron when six of the nine Swordfish Is on strength were damaged in a severe gale. The squadron attempted to leave Crail for Twatt in the Orkney Islands on 26th January, but bad weather delayed the move until the following day.

The Swordfish Is of 833 Squadron followed those of 819 Squadron from Lee-on-Solent to Crail on 5th February 1942, the intention being to deploy the unit in the ill-fated escort carrier HMS *Dasher*. After training at Crail, 833 Squadron continued to work up at Hatston in the Orkney Islands and Machrihanish before embarking in HMS *Biter* and deploying for service in North African skies. The day before 833 Squadron's departure, another Swordfish unit arrived at Crail. This was 822 Squadron, a TBR unit under the command of Maj A. R. Burch and equipped with nine Swordfish Is. Destined to serve in HMS *Biter* before the carrier returned to Great Britain, the squadron was re-equipped at Crail with the Albacore I. A brief work-up on their new aircraft was achieved at Crail before the unit moved the short distance to Donibristle and eventual service aboard HMS *Furious*.

Although it was not the domain of the RAF, torpedo-dropping was a role that the Handley Page Hampden had inherited since its removal from front-line RAF Bomber Command operations. The Hampden TB.I was well suited to the task and during early 1942 a few squadrons were

No. 785 Squadron began to receive the Barracuda from late 1942, continuing to operate the type until the unit's disbandment in 1946. (Dennis Philips via R. C. Sturtivant)

formed for anti-shipping operations. Three of these squadrons were located in Scotland, the nearest being 144 Squadron which arrived at Leuchars in April 1942. By the end of the year two more Hampden TB.I-equipped units, the Canadian-manned 415 (Swordfish) Squadron and the Australian-manned 455 Squadron, would pass through Leuchars. All three squadrons were conveniently placed to detach aircraft to Crail for training purposes and continued to do so until at least September 1942. While none of the RAF aircraft were based at Crail, they were a common sight at the base and would often fly in from Leuchars in the morning then were gone again by the same evening.

Two Hampdens were lost whilst operating from Crail during 1942. The first incident, in June, involved an aircraft of 144 Squadron which crashed near the airfield because of engine failure; the Canadian crew all escaped unhurt. The second incident, on 16th July, was more serious. Sergeant R. D. Wells RAAF of 455 Squadron was on approach to land when his Hampden I (P2145) stalled and spun into the ground after an engine cut. Wells died later of his injuries but his passenger, Sgt Dawboan RAAF, escaped with his life.

At nearby Dunino, the airfield's undulating grass runways were not coping well with periods of heavy rain. To make matters worse, the resident unit, the Polish-manned 309 (Ziema Czerwienska) Squadron, was re-equipping with the North American Mustang I. The American fighter was struggling with the conditions at Dunino and so it was decided to move 'B' Flight to Crail on 15th June 1942. It was during 309 Squadron's stay at Crail that a very interesting sortie took place.

While the Mustang's range was impressive for a single-seat, single-engined fighter, it was widely believed that the aircraft could not be flown to Norway and back without running out of fuel. Accordingly, all of the RAF's Mustang-equipped units at the time were strictly prohibited from attempting to reach Norway. However, the Polish keenness for seeing action would prevail and one of 309 Squadron's pilots, Flt Lt J. Lewkowicz, a fully qualified aeronautical engineer, calculated that the Mustang could indeed be flown to Norway and back. He presented his findings to Group Headquarters which duly dismissed them. Refusing to taking no for an answer, Flt Lt Lewkowicz undertook an unauthorised flight to Norway, strafed some military installations and returned to Dunino safely. The flight became legendary overnight amongst Polish airmen, not to mention the Allies as a whole. Although Lewkowicz was reprimanded for breaking just about every rule in the book, he was also heartily congratulated for his efforts by Air Marshal Sir Arthur Barratt KCB, CMG, MC, AOC Army Co-Operation Command. Almost overnight, the role of the Mustang was re-evaluated because of Lewkowicz's epic flight. Not long thereafter, the Polish airmen of 'B' Flight rejoined their unit and went into action over occupied Europe.

From December 1942, both 785 and 786 Squadrons began to receive the Fairey Barracuda carrier-based torpedo bomber. Initially, only a handful of Barracuda Is arrived (just 30 were built), this model being fitted with a 1,260 hp Rolls-Royce Merlin engine. The ubiquitous Barracuda II, 1,688 of which were built, quickly replaced the seriously underpowered Mk I. Fitted with a more powerful 1,640 hp Merlin 32, the first of many Barracuda IIs began to arrive at Crail from April 1943 for 785 Squadron. Whereas 785 Squadron continued to operate its Swordfish Is and IIs and Albacore Is alongside the Barracudas, 786 Squadron retired their Swordfish and Albacores within weeks of the Barracudas arriving. By the war's end, 785 Squadron had over 50 Barracuda IIs and 786 Squadron a remarkable 80 examples on strength.

As with virtually all FAA and carrier-based aircraft, the Barracuda's general appearance was dictated by functionality. Very few naval aircraft were pleasing to look at and the Barracuda was no exception. The single-engined torpedo bomber was of all-metal construction and carried a three-man crew beneath a long, 'greenhouse'-type canopy. The aircraft was fitted with a thick-cord shoulder wing, a 'T'-shaped tail and a spider-like undercarriage, all of which added to its already unusual appearance. The wing design was heavily dictated by the fit of the Fairey-Youngman dive flaps which made the aircraft very stable when diving from altitude. Defensive armament was simply a pair of Vickers 'K' guns in the rear cockpit, but the Barracuda could also carry a variety of underwing stores or a single 1,620 lb torpedo.

Dive-bombing was a new art which needed to be taught to the trainee Barracuda crews. Targets were towed behind ships for the aircrews to bomb, and these training sorties were supported by many hours in the classroom and on the numerous synthetic trainers which were available at Crail. One of the most impressive simulators was the Torpedo Attack Trainer (TAT), which consisted of a huge hemispherical screen measuring 40 ft across, onto which were projected the images of enemy ships. The pupil pilot was located in the middle of the room inside a Link Trainer facing the screen. Above him was a large rotatable platform fitted with various lamps and an epidiascope, which projected the image of the ship by using models only a few inches long. As the pupil manoeuvred his simulated aircraft, the ship's position would respond accordingly. Once a torpedo was 'launched', a white line of light showed its track and, if the ship stopped on the line, the instructor would confirm a hit. The various lights and lanterns above the pupil could represent just about any weather condition to add even more realism to the exercise. A separate lantern fitted under the Link Trainer could even replicate various water effects, from a mill pond sea to large waves.

By now, operational training consisted of seven weeks at Crail which involved learning to drop torpedoes, followed by three weeks of deck-landing training to Royal Navy standards at Arbroath.

Albacore and Swordfish squadrons continued to pass through Crail during late 1942. Tragically, 786 Squadron lost one of its valued and highly experienced instructors, Lt H. de G. Hunter DSC, on 5th November when his Albacore I (N4357) crashed into the Firth of Forth only moments after demonstrating a practice torpedo attack. Lt Hunter had earned his DFC whilst piloting one of fourteen Swordfish Is that took off from HMS *Ark Royal* on the night of 26th May 1941 to attack and disable the German battleship *Bismarck*. The damage inflicted by the torpedo-carrying Swordfish during repeated attacks allowed the heavy cruiser HMS *Dorsetshire* to finish off the German battleship with a single torpedo the following day.

The Fleet Air Arm Mobile Workshop unit was formed at Crail

The last unit to be reformed at Crail during the Second World War was 711 Squadron, initially with the Barracuda II.

during early 1943. The unit operated between Dunino and Crail until mid-1944, by which time established servicing was in place.

A third permanent unit joined 785, 786 and 770 Squadrons at Crail on 5th March 1943 when 778 Squadron, a Service Trails Unit squadron, brought its collection of aircraft from Arbroath, all under the command of Lt Cdr H. J. F. Lane. Originally formed at Lee-on-Solent in September 1939, the unit's role was to carry out Service trials on all new types of naval aircraft entering service during 1941 and 1942. These included the Chesapeake I, Kingfisher I, Barracuda I and early Marks of the Seafire, plus any equipment supporting these aircraft types. Equipment testing carried out at Crail included evaluation of aerial mines and flame floats, the latter being designed to ignite on contact with the water. The squadron was also the first unit to bring the Grumman Avenger I to Crail, having been the first FAA unit to receive the big, American-built torpedo bomber back in 1942. The Avenger was a popular aircraft with its crews and was one of the most stable platforms ever built for the delivery of a torpedo. Out of the 9,839 built, 958 served with the FAA from 1943 onwards, many seeing action in the Far East.

For anyone who served with 770 Squadron, mention of the Chesapeake I would probably not bring back pleasant memories. In what proved to be a particularly bad year for the squadron, five of these two-seat dive-bombers were lost, all of them in fatal accidents. The first loss occurred on 30th January, when Lt J. Wilson force-landed his aircraft (AL940) into the sea. Sadly, neither Lt Wilson nor his passenger, Leading Photographer F. Chuter were able to escape the aircraft before it slipped beneath the waves. The second accident occurred when Sub Lt J. Thorpe stalled his aircraft (AL928) whilst involved in co-operation work with local anti-aircraft guns and crashed just north of Crail village. His passenger, Air Mechanic 1st Class J. Harris from 786 Squadron, perished in the crash.

Worse was to come on 27th April when yet another 770 Squadron Chesapeake I (AL938) not only claimed the lives of its two crewmen but also many more on the ground. Whilst carrying out practice dummy dive-bombing attacks at Ferny Ness Point, Sub Lt K. Joll appeared unable to pull out of his dive during the second such attack and crashed directly in front of a Scottish Motor Traction bus filled with personnel travelling from the range. The Chesapeake bounced in a ball of flame and crashed straight into the bus. Both Sub Lt Joll and Leading Telegraphist Air Gunner (TAG) R. Hartley in the Chesapeake and the bus driver were killed instantly; a further ten naval ratings and a US Navy seaman aboard the bus were either killed outright or died of their injuries not long thereafter. It is possible that the pilot had been incapacitated because of carbon monoxide fumes entering the cockpit. The official inquiry into the incident criticised the total lack of emergency services and first aid on hand which could have saved some of those seriously injured in the bus.

Another low-level practice attack, this time on anti-aircraft guns positioned on the edge of the airfield, claimed the lives of Sub Lt Ray and Leading Photographer G. Strachan when their aircraft (AL937) crashed on the rocky foreshore at Fife Ness Reach on 20th July 1943. The fifth fatal accident involved Sub Lt G. Danby and his passenger, Leading TAG McEntree. In circumstances similar to those that had claimed AL940 and its two crewmen back in January, Sub Lt Danby attempted to ditch his aircraft (AL915) in the sea, but both crewmen perished when the Chesapeake crashed a mere one and a half miles from the airfield.

By late 1943 the Barracuda torpedo bomber was a common sight at Crail, but it was not until 18th October that the first operational squadron equipped with the type arrived. The unit in question was 810 Squadron, under the command of Lt Cdr(A) A. J. B. Forde, which arrived from the carrier HMS *Illustrious* after serving in the Mediterranean. The unit's stay at Crail lasted a mere three weeks before it moved to Machrihanish for a weapons training refresher course prior to re-embarking in HMS *Illustrious* in late November.

Another short-term resident was 811 Squadron, which formed a new Fighter Flight at Crail on 25th November 1943. The squadron's main equipment at this time was the Swordfish II, but the new flight was equipped with Grumman Wildcat IVs. The unit departed for Stretton in Lancashire on 10th December 1943.

Crail's long association with 770 Squadron came to an end on 29th January 1944, but the unit only moved as far as Dunino and its aircraft were still quite often seen at Crail until 770 Squadron was disbanded in October 1945. The squadron's poor safety record, especially with regard to the Chesapeake I, later prompted a Court of Enquiry which concluded that part, if not all, of the blame should fall on the squadron's longest-serving commanding officer, Lt Cdr(A) A. F. E. Payen.

Early 1944 saw the comings and goings of several operational units, the majority of them equipped with Barracudas. The most notable of these were 820 and 826 Squadrons, which stayed at Crail from February to June 1944. Both squadrons, after leaving for HMS

Indefatigable, were involved in an unsuccessful torpedo attack on the German battleship *Tirpitz* at anchorage in Alta Fjord in Norway during August 1944.

The departures from Crail continued on 15th August 1944, when 778 Squadron moved to Arbroath where it continued to undertake trials of more new aircraft types planned for service with the FAA.

The last unit to arrive at Crail during the Second World War was 711 Squadron, which reformed at the airfield on 9th September 1944. Originally formed as a Catapult Flight in 1936 operating the Hawker Osprey III and Supermarine Walrus I, the unit was reformed as a Torpedo Training Squadron equipped with Barracuda IIs plus a few Stinson Reliant Is in support and commanded by Lt Cdr(A) J. B. Curgenven-Robinson DSC.

By this stage of the war, 786 Squadron was training crews on anti-submarine courses and Barracuda familiarisation. By the end of 1944, the squadron had become part of 1 Naval Operational Training Unit (OTU) and, with the end of hostilities in Europe, started to receive Avengers. No.711 Squadron had become an Avenger OTU by August 1945 but this task rapidly reduced and the unit disbanded into 785 Squadron on 21st December 1945. No.786 Squadron was reduced and also disbanded into 785 Squadron the same day.

Despite the swelling in size of 785 Squadron, the need for torpedo bomber crews and indeed for such a method of attack had long since passed. Having served at Crail for five and a half years, 786 Squadron disbanded on 1st March 1946.

The airfield itself was now rapidly running down and the last FAA flying unit to pass through Crail was a small group of Airspeed Oxford Is from 780 Squadron. The unit, which had reformed as an Advanced Flying Training Unit on 28th March 1946, arrived from Hinstock in Shropshire in December 1946 for instrument training. They moved to Donibristle on 27th March 1947 but continued to fly circuits at Crail until 23rd May 1947.

On 28th April 1947, Crail airfield ceased to be HMS *Jackdaw*, becoming HMS *Bruce* for ground training purposes. The main task of this new establishment was as a boys' training establishment, and over 1,300 passed through HMS *Bruce* during the late 1940s and early 1950s in preparation for joining the senior service. During this period the airfield gained a giant replica tall ship's mast, which was duly located next to the parade ground. The base and approximately ten feet of the mast are all that remain of the structure today.

Aircraft briefly returned to Crail in the 1950s when 1830 Squadron

This aerial view gives an idea of how many wartime buildings are still standing on the airfield, and the excellent preserved condition of the runways, perimeter track and dispersal roads.

moved from Donibristle with Fairey Fireflies. The squadron, which used the airfield for circuit training, was active at Crail from December 1950 through to November 1952. By then the Army had taken over the site, with the 1st Battalion The Black Watch taking up residence. It was at Crail that they were mobilized before being deployed to fight in the Korean War. They returned in 1955 but left for good to serve in British Guiana not long thereafter.

The final use of Crail by a military aviation unit occurred between March 1953 and August 1957. Initially moved because of extension work being undertaken at Leuchars, the St Andrews University Air Squadron continued to make use of Crail's quiet runways for many years after the work at Leuchars had been completed. The airfield also housed the Joint Services School for Linguists from 1956 to 1960. The school taught members from all three armed services mainly Eastern Block languages such as Russian, Polish and Czech. At the height of the Cold War, these personnel were employed to listen in on all Soviet communications.

The first of several sales to return the land occupied by Crail airfield to civilian use began in 1961. By 1963, all of these plots of land had been returned to their original owners or purchased by others. The airfield has been used for a variety of different tasks since it became civilianised. Farming dominates, and several film companies have used the surviving hangar over the years. The runways have been

The three-storey control tower dominates the airfield with the unique Aircraft Repair Shed visible in the background. (Author)

used for motor sport and a permanent go-karting circuit is in situ today. The runways also provide a good location for Sunday markets.

With little exception, the runways, perimeter track and dispersal areas remain today and are overlooked by the impressive three-storey control tower, which has defiantly stood the test of time. The World War Two Bellman hangars have long since found new homes elsewhere or been scrapped, but the single Aircraft Repair Shed remains in use. Behind the control tower, one can see row upon row of buildings, very few of which are nearing dereliction. The TAT, to name just one building, still exists, complete with much of its original equipment. Altogether over 150 buildings remain, the majority of which are still in a usable condition. This makes Crail the best-preserved disused Second World War airfield in Scotland, and possibly one of the most impressive in Great Britain too.

3
DONIBRISTLE

Affectionately known as 'Donibee' by the many thousands of military personnel and civilian workers who passed through it, Donibristle had a diverse history which dated back to 1917 and continued, almost uninterrupted, for a further 42 years. Industry and housing have virtually removed it from today's aviation map but its memory will live on as one of Scotland's earliest airfields.

The explanation for an airfield being built on the northern edge of the Firth of Forth, on rising ground above Dalgety Bay, can be traced back to 1903. It was then that the decision was made to build a new naval dockyard at Rosyth, upstream from the Forth Railway Bridge. Construction began in 1909, but it was March 1916 before the work was fully completed and Rosyth Naval Dockyard was deemed ready for operational use.

During the early stages of the First World War, the Admiralty viewed aircraft as nothing more than a novelty; but as the conflict developed and spread, their importance and operational value to naval operations, especially in support of warships, grew rapidly. As a consequence, in late 1916 various sites surrounding Rosyth were inspected and surveyed for the location of a landing ground and eventual storage area for large numbers of aircraft belonging to the Royal Naval Air Service (RNAS).

In early 1917, as part of the aerial defence of the Firth of Forth and Edinburgh, 77 (Home Defence) Squadron of the Royal Flying Corps (RFC) established a small emergency landing ground on land belonging to the Earl of Moray at Donibristle House. The Earl was none too happy about aircraft using his land, but the commanding officer of 77 Squadron was a good friend and coaxed him round to the idea. Several trees had to be removed to clear a runway, after which a single guard hut and a few ancillary buildings were constructed.

Not a single aircraft used the small landing ground before the arrival of the RNAS in August 1917. Allocated to the Admiralty on 17th September 1917, work soon began on building a large aircraft repair depot. Several large aircraft sheds, each measuring 200 ft long and 100 ft wide, were built on the northern side of the landing ground. These sheds were needed to provide protection for up to 50 aircraft from the elements while they were prepared for use by the Grand Fleet in the spring of 1918. This task brought about the formation of the Fleet Aircraft Acceptance Depot in October 1918, which was renamed the Fleet Aircraft Repair Depot not long thereafter. The importance of Donibristle's first major role was reflected in the fact that the airfield was kept open after the Armistice and continued to overhaul carrier-based aircraft until 1921, when it was reduced to Care and Maintenance.

The airfield was reopened in 1924 as a shore base for Fleet Air Arm (FAA) aircraft leaving carriers anchored in the Firth of Forth. The Coastal Defence Torpedo Flight was formed here on 7th July 1928 and redesignated 36 Squadron three months later; the first of several RAF torpedo-bomber units that passed through Donibristle during the late 1920s and 1930s with Hawker Horsleys and Vickers Vildebeests. Many of the units at the airfield took part in trials and exercises with Rosyth-based warships. It is also worth noting that the RAF established a seaplane station east of Inverkeithing Bay during the 1930s. Built with six mooring places, it was not in use by the beginning of the Second World War, but 948 (Balloon) Squadron did make use of it from October 1939 to early 1942.

Initially built on land loaned and then purchased by the Air Ministry, Donibristle airfield was officially transferred to the Admiralty on 24th May 1939 and commissioned as HMS *Merlin*. Despite being upgraded and used continuously by FAA squadrons since the First World War, this was in fact the first time that the Royal Navy had complete control of the airfield. Donibristle was one of five airfields handed over to the Royal Navy at the time and the only one of the five in Scotland.

The first task for HMS *Merlin* was the formation of at least two new Deck Landing Training (DLT) squadrons. The first of these, 767 Squadron, was formed at Donibristle on 24th May 1939 by renumbering 811 Squadron and was equipped with Fairey Swordfish Is and Albacore Is, Blackburn Shark IIs and a de Havilland Moth. The unit took part in several DLT detachments aboard HMS *Furious* before it found itself on operational service in the Mediterranean by 1940, aboard HMS *Argus*.

The second of Donibristle's DLT units was 769 Squadron, formed as a Fighter DLT Squadron by renumbering 801 Squadron, and equipped with Blackburn Skua IIs and Roc Is and Gloster Sea Gladiators. Like 767 Squadron, the unit carried out the majority of its training from the deck of HMS *Furious* before four of its Sea Gladiators formed 804 Squadron at Hatston in the Orkney Islands on 30th November 1939. The following day, 769 Squadron was disbanded.

Having been associated, since the end of the First World War, with the overhaul and storage of aircraft, it was a logical step for Donibristle to become a Royal Naval Aircraft Repair Yard during the Second World War. Located on the north-western side of the airfield, the new yard, virtually the equivalent of a Naval Dockyard, was autonomous from the rest of the airfield. The repair yard was not under the control of HMS *Merlin* and throughout the war years and beyond, relied heavily on the employment of local civilians. Its main task was to carry out major maintenance on all types of FAA aircraft, with minor or basic maintenance still being carried out by the surrounding RNAS stations. As the war progressed, aircraft carriers that arrived at Rosyth and other dockyards in Scotland delivered battle-damaged aircraft for repair to Donibristle. By 1941, the latter work made up one third of all tasks assigned to the repair yard. Most of the damage that was repaired had been sustained during flying accidents rather than as a result of enemy action.

During 1940, the repair yard at Donibristle employed at least 450 civilians and over 500 military personnel; the latter by now were mainly comprised of Royal Navy engineers, the RAF having moved out by the beginning of 1940. The numbers employed by the repair yard increased rapidly to approximately 2,000 civilians and over 1,000 military personnel by the end of 1944.

From the outbreak of the war, the repair yard was also employed to overhaul aircraft engines. The first such was the 775 hp Bristol Pegasus, as fitted to the Supermarine Walrus amphibian. The first Pegasus unit to be overhauled was fitted to a Walrus at Donibristle which was then flown to Hatston where it joined the seaplane carrier HMS *Pegasus*. More Bristol units were taken on in 1940, including examples of the 890 hp Perseus XII for the Skua II and the 840 hp Mercury VIIIA for the Sea Gladiator. As the war progressed, an increasingly diverse range of engines was catered for. These included the 1,065 hp Bristol Taurus II and 1,130 hp Taurus XII that powered the Albacore I; and various models of the Rolls-Royce Merlin and Griffon that powered variants of the Fairey Barracuda and Fairey Firefly respectively during the later years of the war. American-built engines were also transported to Donibristle for overhaul. Initially these were examples of the troublesome 1,240 hp Wright Cyclone G-205A, as fitted to the Grumman Martlet I; there then followed the more reliable 2,250 hp Pratt and Whitney R-2800 engine that powered the Grumman Hellcat and Chance Vought Corsair.

By the war's end, over 7,000 aircraft had passed through the repair yard at Donibristle. This figure was made up of over 80 different aircraft types, all of which were operated by the FAA with the exception of a few RAF Hawker Typhoons.

Donibristle's role as a temporary shore base for carrier-based squadrons began to gain momentum from early 1940 onwards. Throughout the war the airfield was also the starting point for many FAA squadrons which were forming or reforming, a good example being 801 Squadron which reformed at Donibristle on 15th January 1940. Under the command of Lt Cdr H. P. Bramwell and equipped with six Skua IIs, by 2nd February 1940 801 Squadron had moved to Evanton for armament training. In April 1940 the squadron's Skuas and aircrews were involved in Norwegian operations from the carrier HMS *Ark Royal*. The unit's short stay at Donibristle following reformation was typical of the many 'here today, gone tomorrow' squadrons which passed through the airfield during the war years.

During 1940, no less than thirteen FAA units passed though Donibristle before the first and only long-term resident squadron to be based at the airfield was formed. The unit in question was 782 Squadron, which was reformed on 1st December 1940 at Donibristle under the command of Lt Cdr(A) A. Goodfellow. Originally formed in October 1939, 782 Squadron briefly served as an Armament Training squadron, the intention being that it would operate Fairey Swordfish. However, before any aircraft were delivered, the original unit was disbanded and amalgamated into 774 Squadron.

The new 782 Squadron was reformed from a Communication Flight at Donibristle which was originally established on 1st July 1940 by crews from Jersey Airlines. Also known as the Northern Communications Squadron, 782 Squadron was initially equipped with a selection of aircraft which, in addition to more familiar types such as the Albacore I, Swordfish I, Roc I and Skua II, included examples of the de Havilland DH.86, Percival Proctor IA, Fairey Seal I and the Royal

Two officers pose in front of de Havilland Flamingo BT312, with its original 782 Squadron name of Merlin VI. *(via R. C. Sturtivant)*

Navy's only example of the DH.95 Flamingo. Originally designed and built as a twin-engined small airliner, three Flamingos were taken over by the RAF for use as communications and light transport aircraft. The example acquired by the Royal Navy (BT312) was converted by de Havillands at Hatfield and delivered to Donibristle on 30th November 1940. Like all of 782 Squadron's aircraft, the name *Merlin* was painted on the forward fuselage and the Flamingo was given the name *Merlin VI*. As 782 Squadron's fleet of aircraft increased in number, the Flamingo was eventually rebadged as *Merlin 27*, the change of name giving a clear indication of just how many aircraft were then in service with the unit.

The main role of 782 Squadron was to establish regular scheduled flights between isolated naval airfields in mainland Scotland, the Shetland Islands, the Orkney Islands and Northern Ireland. Later, long routes down the west coast of Great Britain terminated at Lee-on-Solent in Hampshire. These flights, usually undertaken in the four-engined DH.86, would take up to five hours' flying time and involved stops at Abbotsinch, Machrihanish, Aldergrove in Northern Ireland, Ronaldsway (Isle of Man), Burscough in Lancashire, Culham in Oxfordshire and finally Lee-on-Solent.

By 1941 the Albacore, Swordfish, Seal and Roc had fallen by the wayside as more suitable transport aircraft arrived for use by 782 Squadron. One such type was the de Havilland DH.89M Dominie I, a military conversion of the highly successful twin-engined Rapide biplane, the first example of which for 782 Squadron was delivered to Donibristle in July 1941. The highly capable Rapide remained with the squadron until it disbanded in 1953, making it not only the longest-serving aircraft type for 782 Squadron but also for the Royal Navy at that time. A single example of the Percival Q.6 Petrel also arrived in 1941, as did single examples of the de Havilland Moth and Tiger Moth II.

Another aircraft type delivered to 782 Squadron during 1941 was the Handley Page Harrow, several transport-configured examples of which arrived for the unit in June that year. Officially known as the Harrow Transport but more often referred to as the 'Sparrow', this troop carrier was a conversion of the pre-war Harrow twin-engined bomber that involved the removal of its gun turrets and the addition of a new, streamlined nose. With seats fitted, up to 30 passengers could be carried; but the Sparrow's size meant that it was also capable of carrying larger items for supply such as aircraft engines. Sparrows served with 782 Squadron from June 1941 to July 1943, but on 15th February 1943 the unit suffered its most serious accident with a Sparrow when one of the aircraft on strength (K6946) was lost whilst

Originally built as a Handley Page Harrow II bomber, K7001 was converted to a Sparrow transport and served with 782 Squadron Donibristle as Merlin XVII.

flying from Wick to Lossiemouth. It was presumed that the aircraft crashed or unsuccessfully tried to ditch into the sea not long after departing Wick. Tragically, all three crew and 27 passengers were lost; only the body of a Wren was ever found.

January 1942 saw the arrival of a Percival Vega Gull for 782 Squadron and, in June 1942, the start of another long association with an aircraft type when the first Airspeed Oxford I for the unit arrived. Examples of the very useful twin-engined Oxford remained in service with 782 Squadron until April 1953.

Delivery of the Stinson Reliant I in December 1943 marked the beginning of a wave of American-built types for 782 Squadron. Next came examples of the twin-engined Beech Expediter C.2 and C.1, in May and October 1944 respectively. Another Beech twin, the Traveller I staggered-wing biplane, joined the fleet in June 1944. These American types were complemented during 1944 by 782 Squadron's most capable transport aircraft to date, the Douglas Dakota. Frustratingly for the crews of the squadron, only a single Dakota C.III (FD904) was delivered, there being an urgent need for transport aircraft elsewhere as the Allies began the slow advance eastwards to Berlin. Post-war, no fewer than seventeen variants of seven different aircraft types that included ex-FAA fighters such as the Firefly, Seafire and Sea Fury were assigned for use by 782 Squadron before the unit was disbanded at Donibristle on 9th October 1953.

Having been steadily upgraded and expanded as the war progressed and the workload at Donibristle increased, by late 1943 the airfield boasted a pair of new tarmac runways which replaced the original grass ones. Restrictions on space and the nature of the surrounding terrain made positioning of the runways very difficult. The new main runway roughly ran from east to west and was only 970 yds long but, unusually for a naval runway, was 50 yds wide (20 yds wider than the standard RNAS runway). Despite its relatively modest length it was still over 300 yds longer than the original grass runway it replaced and was complemented by a second runway which measured 800 yds in length. However, the second runway was almost surplus to requirements because its alignment differed from that of the new main runway by only a few degrees.

A maze of perimeter tracks connected the two runways with dispersal areas. Four new Bellman hangars were constructed on the south side of the airfield, in addition to three Bessoneau hangars. The Bessoneau design dated from the First World War, and with its wooden structure and canvas covering, was designed to be re-erected

A pair of de Havilland Dominies, Merlin I *and* IX, *with one of Donibristle's hangars in the background plus a pair of Sea Hurricanes. (via R. C. Sturtivant)*

by twenty skilled men in 48 hours. Large dispersal areas were built further down the seashore at Dalgety Bay and facilities were expanded in this area for the air gunnery department. Gun butts for testing guns and a fully operational bomb dump were also built, the latter being necessary should an operational squadron arrive and need rearming before their return to a carrier or transfer to another shore base.

Before the end of the Second World War, approximately 56 FAA squadrons passed through Donibristle. Many of them returned several times and a large proportion were operational units. Initially, many of these were equipped with Swordfish, one of the early significant arrivals being 'X' Flight of 821 Squadron with six Swordfish Is which arrived from Hatston on 2nd December 1940. This small unit had already seen a lot of action, including the distinction of carrying out the first daylight torpedo attack of the Second World War. The target was the German battleship *Scharnhorst,* which was attacked in daylight off the Norwegian coast on 21st June 1940, but on this occasion the brave Swordfish crews were unsuccessful.

Other Swordfish-equipped units that spent time at Donibristle included a detachment of 825 Squadron from Arbroath in March 1941 and 819 Squadron from Hatston for three weeks in March 1942. Formation of the FAA's last operational Swordfish squadron took place at Donibristle on 15th June 1943. The unit, 860 Squadron, was unusual in that it was formed as a Royal Netherlands Navy-manned Torpedo Bomber Reconnaissance squadron with half of the initial personnel coming from Holland. Under the command of Lt J. van der Toorren, RNethN, the unit received its first six Swordfish Is four days after forming. One month later, on 19th July, 860 Squadron left Donibristle to continue their training at Hatston. A further eight Swordfish squadrons passed through Donibristle, the last of which, 816 Squadron, which also operated the Grumman Wildcat V, left for Machrihanish on 17th April 1944.

Four Albacore-equipped squadrons also passed through Donibristle between March 1941 and June 1942. First to arrive was 828 Squadron from Campbeltown for four days in March, followed by 827 Squadron from Machrihanish for three weeks in June, 817 Squadron from HMS *Victorious* for two weeks in October and finally 822 Squadron from Crail for just over a month in May/June 1942.

Fighter-equipped FAA squadrons were also regular visitors from the beginning of the Second World War, with units equipped with the Grumman Martlet, Hawker Sea Hurricane, Supermarine Spitfire and Seafire and Chance Vought Corsair commonplace. Another FAA fighter to be seen at Donibristle was the Fairey Fulmar; the first carrierborne aircraft to be armed with eight machine guns. With

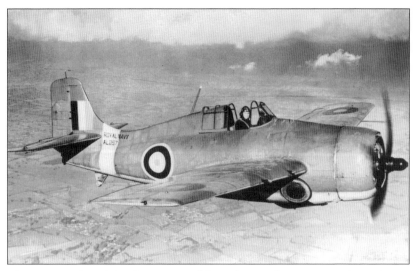

The FAA version of the Grumman Wildcat, the Martlet was a regular visitor to Donibristle.

similar proportions to those of the Fairey Battle light bomber, the Fulmar I was fitted with a 1,080 hp Rolls-Royce Merlin VIII engine; this was replaced in the Fulmar II by the more powerful 1,300 hp Merlin XXX, but even so the Mk II could still only manage a maximum speed of 280 mph. Despite this, the Fulmar served the FAA well and five operational units equipped with the big fighter passed through. Two of them, 884 and 808 Squadrons, were reformed at Donibristle; two more, 886 and 893 Squadrons, were formed there. The last of these four units, which was also equipped with the Martlet, used Fulmars as a temporary measure and was quite possibly the last squadron to receive the type. The last operational Fulmars left Donibristle on 23rd August 1942.

The seemingly never-ending task of destroying the German battleship *Tirpitz* continued into 1944. The combined efforts of the RAF and FAA were used in Operation *Tungsten* and many of the squadrons involved were prepared at Donibristle. The operation was planned for 1st April 1944 and two of the FAA units which took part, 827 and 830 Squadrons, arrived at Donibristle from the carrier HMS *Furious* on 7th April. Both squadrons were equipped with Barracuda IIs and their involvement in the attack, while not responsible for sinking the *Tirpitz*, was a major contributory factor in the battleship's eventual demise. The two Barracuda squadrons returned to HMS *Furious* on 20th April 1944.

Attacks on the *Tirpitz* continued throughout the summer of 1944 and involved another three FAA squadrons from Donibristle in Operations *Goodwood I* to *IV*, carried out between 22nd and 29th August. On this occasion, the operation was not as successful as previous attacks and, despite their best efforts, the fate of the *Tirpitz* now rested in the hands of RAF Bomber Command. On 15th September 1944, 27 Lancasters armed with 12,000 lb 'Tallboy' bombs attacked the *Tirpitz* at her anchorage in Alta Fjord. Although this attack did not destroy the *Tirpitz* outright, a single bomb caused sufficient damage for the battleship never to sail again.

The Barracuda IIs of 828 Squadron, accompanied by two fighter escort squadrons during the *Goodwood* operations, arrived at Donibristle on 2nd September 1944. The fighter units, 1841 and 1842 Squadrons, were equipped with an aircraft type new to the airfield; the Chance Vought Corsair. This superb American-built fighter, which first entered FAA service in August 1943, went on to serve with nineteen squadrons. Over 2,000 were ordered for service with the FAA in several different Marks; those arriving at Donibristle were the Mk II.

Powered by a 2,000 hp Pratt and Whitney R-2800-8 Double Wasp engine, the Corsair was capable of speeds of over 400 mph, could operate comfortably at heights of over 35,000 ft and had an impressive range of 1,000 miles. The Corsair certainly impressed all who came into contact with it at Donibristle before the two squadrons returned to HMS *Formidable* on 16th September. Three days earlier, 828 Squadron had left Donibristle for Machrihanish.

Another aircraft type that was new to Donibristle was the Fairey Firefly I, the FAA's replacement for the Fulmar, which first arrived with 1770 Squadron from HMS *Indefatigable* on 25th July 1944 and briefly again on the 31st. Faster and with more powerful armament than the Fulmar, the Firefly was a versatile aircraft that remained in service with the FAA in a number of variants until 1958. Although this first encounter was a brief affair, the presence of the Firefly at Donibristle would become more commonplace during the post-war years as later variants passed through the airfield.

The last FAA squadron aircraft to visit Donibristle during the Second World War belonged to 1820 Squadron, which arrived on 1st December 1944. The unit was equipped with the Curtiss Helldiver dive-bomber and had been struggling to get to grips with it ever since forming on the type at the US Navy base of Brunswick in Maine on 1st April 1944. After losing several Helldivers in fatal accidents but before becoming operational, 1820 Squadron was disbanded at Burscough on 16th December 1944, twelve days after its transfer there following a stay of just three days at Donibristle.

With the end of the war in Europe, the number of aircraft movements through the airfield declined dramatically. Communication flights continued to be flown by 782 Squadron, with only the airfield's Station Flight in residence. The latter was formed in May 1943 with types that included the Swordfish, Tiger Moth, Dominie and Oxford, but it was disbanded by February 1946.

Some carrier-based units came and went from Donibristle, but the airfield was restricted to piston types and these often struggled to land on the short runway. The most common aircraft types seen during the post-war years were the Firefly, Avenger, Seafire and Hawker Sea Fury. The latter was eventually stored in great numbers at the airfield, all awaiting disposal.

Twelve squadrons were briefly based at the airfield during its final years, the last of which, 1830A Squadron, was formed there on 1st October 1952. The squadron operated Firefly T.2s, FR.5s and AS.6s with North American Harvard T.2Bs and T.3s in support. By 1st

A common sight throughout the war years and beyond, the Airspeed Oxford was in regular use by 782 and 739 Squadrons at Donibristle.

November, the unit had left for Abbotsinch, leaving 782 Squadron as the sole flying unit present at Donibristle. This was disbanded on 9th October 1953 and HMS *Merlin* was finally run down and civilianised. The old 782 Squadron was reformed immediately as the Northern Communication Squadron. Now in civilian hands, the aircraft were flown by Airwork pilots and remained active until 1958.

Airwork had also taken over control of the repair yard which was now overhauling examples of the Seafire, Harvard, Sea Fury, Blackburn Firebrand, Douglas Skyraider and Fairey Gannet, as well as Westland Dragonfly and Whirlwind helicopters. By the late 1950s, defence cuts had started to take their toll and Donibristle was earmarked for closure. The last aircraft to be reconditioned at Donibristle was a Douglas Skyraider AEW.1 (WT950) which left for 849 Squadron HQ Flight at Culdrose in Cornwall in January 1959. Three months later, the repair yard and Donibristle airfield were closed down.

Industry and housing have now obliterated the airfield, although the industrial area has incorporated many of the original buildings into its infrastructure. A row of 1920s barrack blocks, neatly lined along Ridge Way are a nice reminder of those peaceful interwar years when biplanes came and went. Roads in the area offer some memory of the

Dominie Air Ambulance X7394 Merlin V of 782 Squadron was tragically lost on 30th August 1946. Whilst en route from Abbotsinch to Stretton, the aircraft flew into Broad Crag, Scafell Pike, killing all six onboard. (via R. C. Sturtivant)

Dominie NF867 had a brief but busy time with 782 Squadron. This photograph was taken at a snow-covered Donibristle during late 1946. (www2images.com)

airfield, with names such as Beech, Fulmar, Taxi and Bellman Way, the last of which refers to the Second World War hangars of which there is now no trace.

Thanks to the efforts of local historian Eric Simpson, a memorial to the men who flew from Donibristle can be found in the local library:

Pause in thy labours for a while
And offer up a silent humble prayer
That they who toiled here once but now are gone
May triumph in the great grim fight
For life and liberty in the world outside.

Lt Brian Sales, Donibristle 1946.

4
DUNINO

Despite a faltering start, the airfield at Dunino was steadily developed throughout the war years. Located five miles due west of Fife Ness and only four miles from the complex airfield at Crail, Dunino would always play second fiddle to the more suitably located coastal airfield.

A new airfield was first surveyed in early 1940 between the tiny village of Beleybridge to the west and the small town of Kingsbarns to the east. A railway line passed through the hamlet of Kilduncan on the eastern perimeter and to the south of this was Kingsbarns railway station. The site was not a natural location for an airfield, being flanked on all sides by ground which rose up to 300 ft above sea level. The main grass runway was 1,400 yds in length, ran from east to west and undulated badly. Two shorter runways crossed it, one measuring 1,200 yds and the other 900 yds in length. During the early months of operations, the runways were the only significant construction on the site. Only a few temporary hutments were also in place by the end of 1940.

Without any kind of formal opening date, Dunino was recognised as a satellite airfield by October 1940, but it was still several months before aircraft would arrive. When Crail opened on 1st October 1940 as HMS *Jackdaw* it, along with the RAF at the time, claimed and possibly used Dunino as a satellite airfield but aviation activity was limited. Crail's two long-term resident units, 785 and 786 Squadrons, claimed Dunino's satellite facilities from their formation in November 1940. However, there is no evidence of them actually using the airfield during the early days of the war.

The first aircraft to seriously make use of Dunino were the Westland Lysanders of 614 (County of Glamorgan) Squadron, an Auxiliary Air

Force unit based at Macmerry in April 1941. At the time, 614 Squadron was converting from the Bristol Perseus XII-powered Lysander II to the Bristol Mercury XX-powered Lysander III so either Mark could have been operating from Dunino at the time. The aircraft were from 'B' Flight of the squadron but it is not clear how long the detachment lasted, though it is possible that the Lysanders were operating in support of locally based Army units.

The first permanent unit to be based at Dunino was the Polish-manned 309 (Ziema Czerwienska) Squadron, who arrived on 8th May 1941 from Renfrew under the command of Cdr Zygmunt Pistl. The unit was formed at Abbotsinch on 8th October 1940 as an army co-operation unit flying the Lysander III and IIIA, the latter Mark arriving at Dunino. The squadron's main work was to support the many Polish Army units based in Scotland at the time and this involved several detachments away from Dunino. These included trips to Longman, Campbeltown and Findo Gask, the last of which was intended as the squadron's final destination. The squadron's stay at Dunino was planned to be temporary; a fact that was reflected in the poor facilities that faced the Poles on their arrival. Not a single permanent building was to be seen and all personnel were initially billeted under canvas. Known by the Poles as 'Bosky Billets', they were all located within woodland (the majority in Kippo Plantation) that surrounded the airfield. Thankfully by September 1941, wooden hutments were being built and the thought of spending a Scottish winter under canvas was removed. Hangars of any kind had yet to be constructed and the Lysanders, which were already struggling with serviceability problems, had to be picketed outside.

The crew of one Lysander IIIA (V9608) had a frightening experience on 18th June 1941. While returning from a local flight and close to home, the aircraft's Very pistol went off in the cockpit. Temporarily blinded and with the cockpit full of smoke, the pilot managed to steer the crippled aircraft towards Dunino. The Lysander was on fire and at the point of breaking up as the pilot successfully crash-landed onto the airfield; both crew escaped relatively unscathed. The Lysander continued to burn furiously; a state of affairs which caused more upset to 614 Squadron's engineers who could only watch as a valuable source of spares was destroyed.

Despite the serviceability problems, 309 Squadron were recorded as being the most reliable of any in Army Co-Operation Command at the time. But it could not and did not last as one after another the tired Lysanders were grounded for a lack of spares. Having no proper

The Lysanders from 'B' Flt, 614 Squadron were the first aircraft to arrive at Dunino in April 1941.

Feeding time for the ground crew of 309 Squadron on a summer's day in 1941. (www.ww2images.com)

The Polish, with 309 Squadron, introduced the North American Mustang I to Dunino in 1942.

hangars in which to conduct major servicing also aggravated the problem; but by early 1942, the first of several Blister hangars were being constructed. Each Blister could only provide cover for a single Lysander but it was better than nothing at all, especially when compared to working on an aircraft in the open with a cold wind blowing.

Each squadron usually had a spare aircraft for communication duties or general flying tasks. In the case of 309 Squadron, the aircraft in question was a de Havilland Tiger Moth which had arrived many months earlier and become a useful machine. On 9th February 1942, with Flg Off Sadowski as pilot and Capt Worledge his passenger, the Tiger Moth departed Dunino for Abbotsinch to attend a meeting in connection with another Polish Army exercise. On the return flight, the little biplane went missing and was sadly confirmed as having crashed into the sea off Toward Point in Argyll, with no sign of the crew.

On 25th February, 309 Squadron suffered its second fatal accident of the month. The aircraft involved was a Lysander IIIA (V9472) being flown by Flg Off P. Dunin and his observer, Flg Off J. Homan. During a practice dive-bombing attack on a gun position near Kenbridge in Fife, Flg Off Dunin left it too late to pull out in the time. The Lysander plunged into the ground, killing both crew instantly and bursting into flames. A subsequent investigation revealed that a control cable had broken giving the pilot no chance of recovering from the dive.

Still struggling along with its now obsolete Lysanders, by early 1942 it was realised by Army Co-Operation Command that their tactics with this aircraft were also obsolete. The Army now needed fast aircraft for tactical photographic reconnaissance at high altitude. The Lysander had neither the speed nor the height and 309 Squadron, like so many others, waited their turn to convert to a new aircraft.

Finally, in April 1942, a signal was received by the squadron that their new aircraft would be the North American Mustang I, and that conversion would begin the following month. Compared to the old Lysander, the Mustang I was approximately 150 mph faster, could fly 10,000 ft higher and travel over 400 miles further. Understandably, the Polish pilots were very excited about their new aircraft. The first small group of pilots travelled to Gatwick in Surrey to begin conversion to the Mustang I. Only a few weeks later, Flt Lt Piotrowski carried out the first operational reconnaissance sortie by a 309 Squadron Mustang I over northern France. Back at Dunino, 'B' Flight of 309 Squadron became the new Mustang I section of the unit, under the command of Flt Lt Piotrowski, receiving its first aircraft on 7th June. 'C' Flight was formed that same month and inherited the Mustang Is which had originally arrived for 'B' Flight. A gunnery course at Inverness in July marked the end of 309 Squadron's association with the Lysander and the unit was declared fully operational on the Mustang I.

By late 1942, Findo Gask's upgrade from a mere Satellite Landing Ground to a fully functioning airfield was complete. In October, almost eighteen months later than originally planned, 309 Squadron began to leave Dunino, the advance parties being followed by 'A' and 'C' Flights on 26th October. 'B' Flight departed on 15th November, destined to become part of 35 Reconnaissance Wing based at Gatwick. By 26th November, all Polish personnel had left Dunino, leaving only a skeleton staffing of RAF airmen at what was now a very quiet airfield.

The Fleet Air Arm (FAA) had not made much use of Dunino since reserving it for its two training squadrons at Crail. Swordfish and Albacores came and went but during 309 Squadron's stay, the Royal Navy tended to operate elsewhere. Aware that 309 Squadron was supposedly not destined to stay at Dunino for very long, the Royal Navy first enquired into the airfield's future in August 1941. Dunino's convenient location as a full satellite airfield for Crail had not gone unnoticed.

The Air Ministry made a verbal offer of the airfield to the Royal Navy in July 1942. The offer was formally accepted by the Royal Navy the following month, but the airfield did not come under the full naval control until the RAF unit had departed. When this finally came about, a naval advance party arrived from Crail on 1st December 1942. The RAF had made its offer of Dunino based on several points, one of which stated that the airfield would be more suited to naval requirements. After only a few days on site, the naval advance party personnel realised that not only was the landing ground very poor, but that any future development plans the Royal Navy had for the airfield should be shelved.

Despite this, the Royal Navy stuck with what they had inherited and on 15th December 1942, Dunino was commissioned as HMS *Jackdaw II*. (The airfield and parent unit at Crail was already commissioned as HMS *Jackdaw I*.) While increasing and enhancing the capability of the airfield was not an option for the Royal Navy, improved facilities were quickly put in place. More brick-built buildings and extra Blister hangars were built. Square dispersals and a perimeter track were also constructed around the airfield and the runways were improved with Steel Matting and Sommerfeld Track.

The first FAA squadron to serve at Dunino arrived on 3rd February 1943. The unit in question was 825 Squadron, under the command of Lt Cdr(A) S. G. Cooper, who brought their Fairey Swordfish Is and IIs from Worthy Down in Hampshire. This highly experienced torpedo bomber squadron had seen a great deal of action since the war began, including a brave attack on the German battleships *Scharnhorst* and *Gneisenau* in February 1942 when all of the squadron's aircraft were lost and the unit's commander, Lt Cdr(A) E. Esmonde, was awarded a posthumous Victoria Cross. By 9th March 1943, the squadron had left Dunino for Machrihanish and then embarked in the carrier HMS *Furious* to undertake anti-submarine operations from Scapa to Iceland.

In early 1943, the FAA still had a training requirement for crews to operate amphibious aircraft from catapults. With this in mind, the one and only squadron to be formed at Dunino was created on 22nd February. Under the command of Lt(A) J. R. Dimsdale, 737 Squadron was formed as an Amphibious Bomber Reconnaissance Training squadron operating the Supermarine Walrus amphibious biplane. Affectionately known as the 'Shagbat', the single-engined Walrus was

Eight FAA squadrons of Swordfish passed through Dunino between February 1943 and July 1944.

a superb multi-role aeroplane which originally entered FAA service in a catapult reconnaissance role. In all, 744 Walrus Is and IIs were built over an eight-year period, which began in 1936. As a Walrus operator, 737 Squadron had a good safety record at Dunino, losing just one aircraft (V2743) when it stalled and spun into the ground near the airfield on 6th April 1943, killing the pilot, Lt M. Liffen.

Swordfish returned to Dunino on 25th February 1943 when three aircraft from 837 Squadron 'A' Flight arrived from Crail. This element of 837 Squadron had been operating from HMS *Argus* on anti-submarine duties off Gibraltar. They were joined by three more Swordfish on 29th March, these aircraft being from 'D' Flight of the same squadron from Hatston in the Orkney Islands. 'D' Flight had recently operated from the escort carrier HMS *Dasher* which tragically blew up two days earlier following a petrol explosion during aircraft refuelling off the Isle of Arran, with the loss of 379 men. All remaining sections of 837 Squadron were reunited at Dunino before departing for Machrihanish on 14th April and a return to the carrier HMS *Argus*.

Another Swordfish-equipped unit, 824 Squadron, arrived from Machrihanish in March 1943 and stayed for a week. They were followed by 827 Squadron on 24th April, the unit being one of the first FAA units to receive examples of the extremely versatile Fairey Barracuda: the first all-metal monoplane carrier-based torpedo bomber built in Great Britain. Under the command of Lt Cdr(A) J. S. Bailey, 827 Squadron received twelve Barracudas in January 1943 and spent most of its time at Dunino carrying out operational training. Part of this training involved night-flying and it was during one such exercise that the squadron recorded its only Barracuda loss at Dunino. While on approach to land, a Barracuda I (P9709) stalled and crash-landed heavily onto the airfield. Luckily, the pilot was not seriously injured and the aircraft was later repaired. The same could not be said of an accident on 12th June, which involved a Barracuda from 778 Squadron on detachment from Crail. The aircraft lost power near the airfield and crash-landed through trees, telephone wires, invasion poles and brick walls before coming to rest. The well-built Barracuda saved the crewmen onboard, but the aircraft was a write-off.

The Barracudas of 827 Squadron had left Dunino by 12th August 1943, once again departing to Machrihanish. Destined to join HMS *Furious*, the squadron would be involved in several attacks on the German battleship *Tirpitz* during 1944. Their place at Dunino was taken three days later by the Swordfish-equipped 860 Squadron from Hatston.

Formed at Donibristle only two months earlier, 860 Squadron was unique within the FAA as being the only unit of its kind to be manned by foreign nationals. The RAF had several such squadrons by this stage of the war, but 860 Squadron, mainly made up of personnel from the Netherlands, was unique. Under the command of Lt J. van der Toorren RNethN, the squadron was formed as a Torpedo Bomber Reconnaissance (TBR) unit equipped with six Swordfish Is. By the time the squadron arrived at Dunino, the unit strength had swelled to nine Swordfish and the Dutch crews were beginning to get to grips with their new aircraft. The squadron lost its first aircraft whilst operating from Dunino on 24th October. The Swordfish in question crashed into the sea off May Island; the pilot managed to escape but his wireless operator, Cpl Van Damm, was presumed drowned. The squadron left Dunino on 3rd November 1943 to begin weapons training at Machrihanish.

The future of 737 Squadron was now beginning to look in doubt as a direct result of naval policy which called for an increase in the number of small escort carriers. This policy had the knock-on effort of reducing the necessity for launching aircraft from catapults. The hammer fell on 28th September 1943 when 737 Squadron was disbanded only months after forming. (The squadron was destined to disband and reform no less than five times before the final end came whilst serving as a Westland Sea King HAS.1 helicopter unit in December 1975.)

Devoid of aircraft for only a few days, the next unit to arrive at Dunino was 833 Squadron from Machrihanish on 6th October 1943. Another Swordfish-equipped unit, the squadron had nine Mk II aircraft on strength under the command of Lt Cdr J. R. C. Callander. Devoid of any particular role, 833 Squadron was selected for Merchant Aircraft Carrier (MAC) operations and moved to Maydown in Northern Ireland on 15th December 1943. The MAC duties never materialised and the squadron was disbanded the following month.

Two days before 833 Squadron's departure, yet another Swordfish-equipped unit, 813 Squadron, took its place at Dunino. This unit, which had already seen a great deal of action during the Second World War, had been reformed at Donibristle on 1st November with nine Swordfish IIs. The squadron used its time at Dunino to work up to an operational state; a goal that was achieved by 20th January 1944, when the unit moved to Inskip in Lancashire.

The last Swordfish unit to serve at Dunino was 838 Squadron which had reformed at Belfast on 1st November 1943 as a TBR squadron. Initially equipped with just four Swordfish IIs aircraft, the fledgling squadron arrived at Dunino on 16th January 1944 after spending a month working with the escort carrier HMS *Nairana* in the Firth of Clyde. The squadron did not remain at Dunino for long and moved to Inskip on 6th February 1944.

By early 1944, Crail, which was not a particularly large airfield, was becoming increasingly overcrowded. To alleviate this situation, one of its long-term resident units, 770 Squadron, was moved the short distance to Dunino on 29th January. Having been reformed as a Fleet Requirements Unit at Donibristle in January 1941, 770 Squadron operated nearly twenty different aircraft types during its four-and-a-half-year existence. On arrival at Dunino, the unit was equipped with the Miles Martinet TT.I target tug and the Vought-Sikorsky Chesapeake I. The latter, known in the United States as the SB2U Vindicator, entered service with the US Navy as a two-seat carrier-borne reconnaissance and dive-bomber aircraft. Although a few of the 50 Chesapeake Is received in October 1940 by the FAA entered front-line service with 811 Squadron, it soon became clear that the type lacked sufficient power to operate from Royal Navy carriers and it was quickly relegated to second-line duties.

During March 1944, 770 Squadron's aircraft strength increased with the arrival of several Bristol Blenheim IVs. The Blenheim was the largest aircraft so far to operate from Dunino and it seemed to cope with the airfield's poor runways quite well. The following month, the unit lost two aircraft, and one of the losses could be directly attributed to the state of the airfield. The accident, on 6th April 1944, involved a Martinet TT.I (MS791) which failed to get airborne because the runway was too boggy. The Martinet crashed into a Nissen hut before exploding in flames, killing the pilot, Sub Lt F. Lawley, instantly. Two Chesapeake Is were also involved in accidents during April; neither was fatal but one involved an engine failure which resulted in the aircraft being written off.

Five aircraft were involved in incidents and accidents at Dunino during May 1944, resulting in a Court of Enquiry being held by the Royal Navy on 5th June 1944. The airfield's general layout and condition was cited as a contributory factor in all of 770 Squadron's problems.

The Hawker Hurricane IIC arrived at Dunino in June 1944, replacing the troublesome Chesapeake Is, but not before the unit lost another of the dive-bombers (AL934) on 27th June. The Chesapeake I was on approach to land at Dunino when, at only 300 ft, it entered a spin and

The Fairey Barracuda II was a common sight at Dunino, especially towards the end of the Second World War. Over 200 were stored in the open, many of them destined to be scrapped where they stood.

crashed. There was no chance of recovery at such a low altitude and the pilot, Sub Lt F. C. Ball, was killed instantly and his observer, W. A. Grossett, died of his injuries not long thereafter.

The last Chesapeake I to serve with the FAA (AL911) had left Dunino by the end of June 1944. Within weeks, and possibly as a direct result of the findings of the Court of Enquiry, 770 Squadron moved to Drem on 25th July 1944.

Despite there no longer being any squadrons based at Dunino, aircraft traffic from Crail was regular and usually consisted of Barracudas in the circuit performing 'touch-and-goes'. After 770 Squadron's departure, the airfield was given a new role to store and maintain surplus aircraft. By this stage of the war, aircraft had become plentiful in number and Dunino's main task was to hold Barracudas. To deal with this, facilities on the airfield were actually expanded and additional Blister hangars and a large Aircraft Repair Shed (ARS) measuring 185 ft long by 110 ft wide were constructed. By the end of the Second World War, over 200 Barracudas were picketed out in the open, side by side at Dunino, all destined to fall under the scrapman's axe.

Only one more operational squadron passed through the airfield before the end of the war and only briefly so. The unit was 820 Squadron, en route from Machrihanish to Lee-on-Solent in Hampshire on 18th October 1944. The unit's Barracudas only stayed for one night, making use of Dunino's facilities before continuing their journey south.

Dunino continued to fill with surplus Barracudas beyond the end of the Second World War. By the time the airfield had reached its storage capacity, the aircraft were being steadily flown out, mainly to Balado Bridge for scrapping. Those airworthy Barracudas still at Dunino were subsequently ferried to Lee-on-Solent and to Stretton in Lancashire, while those that were judged to be unairworthy were broken up on site.

By 1st October 1945, Dunino was under the control of HMS *Merlin*, otherwise known as Donibristle. Dunino was briefly commissioned as HMS *Merlin III* which was amended to *Merlin II* by 6th December. By late 1946, the airfield's storage role had diminished and the Royal Navy began to lease out the land and buildings to interested parties. Despite deciding very early not to retain the airfield, Dunino remained in naval hands until it was fully derequisitioned in 1957.

Although the site has long since returned to agriculture, the layout of the airfield is still intact. All traces of the runways have long since

Several buildings in various states of repair survive at Dunino, the most notable being the airfield's unusual control tower. (Eric Simpson)

disappeared, but remnants of the perimeter track remain. A two-storey control tower still defiantly stands and the frames of several Blister hangars are extant. Wartime buildings in various stages of decay can still be found within the surrounding woodland and on the airfield site itself.

5
GRANGEMOUTH

In the planning for many years prior to its opening, a new airport in the centre of Scotland was a dream come true for many when it first opened in May 1939. Sadly, this well-equipped civilian airfield could not realise its full potential before the outbreak of the Second World War only a few months later.

Envisaged in the late 1920s and proposed in the early 1930s, the construction contracts were not in place until late 1938. Land belonging to Reddoch Farm was surveyed in 1935 as a good location for a new airport, but as the project rumbled on, it was realised that much more land would be needed. By the time work began, 520 acres had been bought from no less than six farmers, of which 280 acres were located within the airfield boundary. Land was acquired from farms at Reddoch, Claret, Wholeflats, Abbotsgrange and Bowhouse plus a large part of Grangemouth golf course.

Work did not begin on the airfield until 9th February 1939, but, within a remarkably short time, Scotland had a new airport. Air Marshal Viscount Trenchard GCB, GCVO, DSO officially opened the fully functioning modern airport on 1st July 1939. Two giant aircraft sheds fronted by a beautiful terminal building dominated Grangemouth. At the front of the terminal was the control tower, which looked out on to a large concrete apron and the runways beyond.

The airport's location was well catered for with a main road running to the north as well as good rail links. Its broader positioning put it directly between Glasgow and Edinburgh with Stirling to the north-west.

Before the official opening, 35 Elementary & Reserve Flying Training School (E&RFTS) was formed at Grangemouth within 50

An almost deserted Grangemouth airport pictured a few weeks before the official opening ceremony. A single 35 E&RFTS Tiger Moth is the only aircraft visible.

(Training) Group on 1st May 1939. Operated by Scottish Aviation Ltd, whose winged tiger's head emblem was prominently displayed in several areas of the airport terminal building, the unit flew the de Havilland Tiger Moth, Avro Anson and Hawker Hind and Audax. The following month, 35 E&RFTS was joined at Grangemouth by 10 Civil Air Navigation School (10 CANS). The new school also came under the control of Scottish Aviation Ltd and operated the Anson I.

On the outbreak of the Second World War, like all the other civilian-operated flying schools, 35 E&RFTS was disbanded. The majority of its aircraft were dispersed to other military units while some were transferred to 10 CANS. The air navigation school continued to operate almost undisturbed but had to make way for regular detachments of Supermarine Spitfire Is from 603 (City of Edinburgh) Squadron based at Turnhouse. Grangemouth was effectively used as a satellite airfield for a single flight of Spitfires which flew to and from the airfield almost every day.

Sadly, whilst operating from Grangemouth, 603 Squadron lost one of its pilots in an avoidable accident. Flg Off J. A. B. Somerville was taxying his Spitfire I (L1047), completely unaware that another Spitfire I (L1059) was landing from behind. Plt Off J. S. Morton landed on top of Somerville's aircraft, killing him instantly and wrecking both fighters.

On the day war broke out, two pilots from 602 (City of Glasgow) Squadron arrived in a Hawker Hart from their home airfield at Abbotsinch. Having just heard Prime Minister Neville Chamberlain's broadcast, they had been ordered to inspect Grangemouth as a potential base to operate from, putting their squadron nearer to the action. Drem, their allocated airfield, was still under Flying Training Command control so, on 7th October 1939, 602 Squadron brought its Spitfire Is to Grangemouth. The unit was only given the opportunity to fly a few defensive patrols from the airfield before Drem became available and the squadron moved again on 13th October.

The Spitfires of 602 and 603 Squadrons had caused quite a stir with the locals, who did not have long to wait before another operational squadron arrived at Grangemouth. There was much expectation and hope pinned on the sleek-looking Spitfire and this would be justified in the months to come. However, the arrival of 141 Squadron did not elicit the same degree of interest, purely because their mount, the Gloster Gladiator I biplane fighter, did not fill the onlookers with the same confidence. Although it was still a capable aircraft, with good performance for a biplane, the reality was that the Gladiator was approaching the end of its operational life.

Having only been formed at Turnhouse a fortnight earlier, personnel were still being posted-in to 141 Squadron during early November 1939. The arrival of the first Bristol Blenheim IFs helped to swell the unit's strength, especially with regard to aircrew. The twin-engined Blenheim had a crew of three compared to the Gladiator's one and demanded more groundcrew and engineers.

On 1st November, 10 CANS was redesignated as 10 Air Observer & Navigation School (AONS), with twelve Anson Is on strength. The school was not destined to stay at Grangemouth much longer and moved to Prestwick on 27th November. For 141 Squadron, this was a protracted working-up period. The unit was given little if no opportunity to have a go at the enemy, its only losses being self-inflicted in several accidents. Its first loss, luckily without injury to the crew, occurred when a Blenheim I (L8688) overshot and crashed through a fence on 15th January 1940.

The squadron departed briefly to Prestwick on 13th February but returned to Grangemouth ten days later. The numbers of Blenheim IFs on strength with the unit had increased by March 1940, but re-equipment was on the horizon again, 141 Squadron having been earmarked to receive the Boulton Paul Defiant I night-fighter; only the second operational unit to receive the type. Deliveries of the new type

The Avro Anson was a familiar sight at Grangemouth when the airport opened. The aircraft operated with 10 CANS and 10 AONS, represented by this wartime camouflaged Anson I.

were slow with only two on strength by the end of April 1940. The same month saw the departure of the last Gladiator I from Grangemouth. The following month, sufficient Defiant Is had arrived for night-fighter operations to begin; but May also saw the first fatal accident on the squadron. On the 15th, Sgt S. F. H. Keene was returning to the airfield when, on joining the circuit at only 700 ft, his Defiant I (L6991) stalled in a very steep turn. The aircraft spun into the ground approximately half a mile south-west of the airfield, killing Keene and his gunner instantly.

By 3rd June 1940, 141 Squadron was finally declared operational on the Defiant I; the last of its Blenheim IFs had already left Grangemouth a few days earlier. Ready for action, the squadron left for Turnhouse on 28th June, but were destined to return to Grangemouth for a short detachment from Prestwick in late July 1940.

Less than three weeks earlier, another Auxiliary Air Force operational unit had made Grangemouth its home. Equipped with Westland Lysander IIs, 614 (County of Glamorgan) Squadron arrived from Odiham in Hampshire on 8th June. The auxiliary army co-operation unit had been specifically moved to Scotland to help with training the many Army units based in the country prior to them being shipped out to the Middle East. Under the command of Wg Cdr D. J. Eyres, 614 Squadron was detached throughout Scotland including trips to Evanton, Montrose, Longman and Dumfries.

The Lysander also took part in many defensive patrols from

Grangemouth covering the east and north-east coast of Scotland, from Berwick-upon-Tweed to Inverness. While minor prangs were fairly common, 614 Squadron only suffered one fatal accident during their time at the airfield. On 10th August 1940, two Lysander IIs flown by Plt Off P. de L. Le Cheminant (N1251) and Flg Off Merrett (P9186) collided in mid-air near Dysart in Fife. Sadly, Merrett and his gunner, Flg Off J. F. Harper, lost control and crashed, killing both men instantly. Plt Off Le Cheminant managed to successfully force-land his damaged aircraft, saving himself and his gunner's life. Le Cheminant survived the war and rose to the rank of Air Vice Marshal, and remained a great advocate for aircraft supporting the Army on the ground.

Fighters returned to Grangemouth in the shape of 263 Squadron on 28th June 1940. The squadron had been virtually wiped out when the carrier HMS *Glorious* was sunk by the German battleships *Scharnhorst* and *Gneisenau* on 8th June. The squadron's Gladiator IIs, along with many air and groundcrew, were lost in the sinking. The squadron was quickly reformed at Drem on 10th June before arriving at Grangemouth with only a few personnel and no aircraft. It was the intention to equip 263 Squadron with the twin-engined Westland Whirlwind I fighter but before they arrived, the unit was given Hawker Hurricane Is as a stopgap measure. The Hurricane Is flew several operational sorties before the first Whirlwind I arrived at Grangemouth on 6th July. Two more arrived on 19th July, by which time 263 Squadron was under the command of Sqn Ldr H. Eeles. It was Sqn Ldr Eeles who delivered the first Whirlwind I (P6966) to Grangemouth having flown the new fighter for a mere 55 minutes at the Westland factory at Yeovil in Somerset!

Because it was the first unit to receive the new fighter, 263 Squadron experienced teething troubles with the type – as had been predicted by the manufacturer. While the Whirlwind was aesthetically very attractive and offered great potential, its main failing was its engines. Westland originally designed the aircraft around a pair of Rolls-Royce Merlins developing at least 1,000 hp each. However, such was the demand for this powerplant, especially for the Hurricanes and Spitfires being built in quantity during the early years of the war, that the Whirlwind had to settle for a pair of 885 hp Rolls-Royce Peregrine I engines. Despite this, at low-level, the Whirlwind I was quick and, fitted with four 20mm cannon in the nose, could pack quite a concentrated punch of firepower. However, the unreliability of the engines, which were not used in any other Service aircraft, continually hampered 263 Squadron's ability to work up on the type. A problem

No.263 Squadron was the first unit to receive the Westland Whirlwind fighter. Several 'teething' problems delayed it from becoming operational and the squadron continued to fly its Hurricanes from Grangemouth.

with the blast of the cannons damaging the nose was quickly rectified and the squadron's aircraft were modified at Grangemouth.

Only two RAF squadrons would ever be equipped with the Whirlwind I which, with its good range and considerable firepower, served on many occasions as a long-range escort fighter as well as a useful ground attack aircraft. For 263 Squadron, use of the Whirlwind I continued until December 1943, when it was replaced by the Hawker Typhoon IB.

July 1940 was a disorganised month for 263 Squadron with the arrival of more 'stopgap' Hurricane Is, the odd Whirlwind and more personnel occurring simultaneously. A handful of Whirlwinds were detached briefly to Montrose to give a few pilots the experience of flying the new fighter. Desperate to have a go at the enemy, two of the squadron's pilots took off without permission in Hurricanes in an attempt to intercept enemy bombers on the night of 13th July. Flt Lt Hull and Flt Lt W. Smith had very little chance of intercepting the enemy in the dark, not even seeing a German aircraft let alone attacking it. Flt Lt Hull managed to recover to Grangemouth safely but Flt Lt Smith, in the other Hurricane I (P2991), quickly became lost in the darkness. Low on fuel, he attempted to make a forced-landing near Carstairs Junction Public School, ten miles south-east of Motherwell. Just as the Hurricane was about to touch down a collision with an unknown obstruction wrecked the fighter. Flt Lt Smith was lucky to escape virtually unhurt from the remains of the Hurricane.

Several other aircraft were involved in accidents off station, the nearest of which occurred on 20th July 1940. Plt Off Downer was tasked with carrying out a local flight when, near to Macmerry, the Merlin engine of his Hurricane I (P2917) started to cut out. Downer quickly attempted a forced-landing in a field approximately one and half miles south-west of Tranent. The Hurricane overshot its intended landing point, struck a hedge and burst into flames. Downer was dragged clear of the blazing fighter but lost his fight for life the following day in a military hospital in Edinburgh.

During August 1940, Whirlwind Is arrived for 263 Squadron in dribs and drabs so that, by the end of the month, only seven were resident at Grangemouth. Ongoing teething troubles reduced the number of aircraft available, as did the loss of the first Whirlwind I (P6966) to have been delivered to the squadron. On 7th August, Plt Off J. McDermott was tasked to carry out a training flight in this aircraft when, during the take-off run, the port mainwheel tyre burst. Plt Off McDermott continued his take-off and climbed away without further incident. However, the tyre blowout was witnessed by several personnel on the ground and the pilot was contacted and told that his undercarriage may have been damaged in the incident. A Hurricane was scrambled to inspect the damage to the Whirlwind and it was quickly realised that it would be too dangerous for Plt Off McDermott to attempt a landing back at Grangemouth. With this in mind, McDermott, with the Hurricane flying in formation, gently circled until he had used up the majority of the Whirlwind's fuel. He then calmly vacated the cockpit, stepped out onto the wing and jumped to safety, landing north of Stirling. The now-powerless and doomed Whirlwind I crashed to the ground near Lanton Farm, Stenhousemuir.

Throughout August, the Hurricane Is of 263 Squadron worked closely with the Lysander IIs of 614 Squadron. The Hurricanes played the role of enemy fighters, giving the Lysander crews valuable experience in how to evade and, in the odd case, actually attack a fighter. Despite being considerably slower and more lightly armed than virtually all of its opponents, the Lysander had the advantage of a superior turning circle. This was often its only chance of survival and if a good pilot could hold the turn tight enough and for long enough, the rear gunner could often get off a shot or two at the enemy.

Still a Hurricane I squadron rather than a fully operational Whirlwind I unit, 263 Squadron left Grangemouth for Drem on 2nd September 1940. The Lysander IIs of 614 Squadron remained at Grangemouth, but were supplemented in November by a flight of Blackburn Rocs which arrived from Odiham in Hampshire. An appeal for pilots to replace those being lost during the Battle of Britain resulted in one of 614 Squadron's pilots and fifteen of the unit's groundcrew volunteering to become aircrew.

Five days after the departure of 263 Squadron, as part of Operation 'Cromwell', 614 Squadron's Lysander IIs were bombed-up in readiness for the anticipated German invasion of Great Britain. Thankfully, due to the efforts of Churchill's 'Few', the church bells never rang out in warning. 'A' Flights of 614 and 4 Squadrons, the latter based at Clifton in Yorkshire, contributed personnel to form a new photo-reconnaissance unit. One unit that benefited from the experience of 614 Squadron's personnel was 241 Squadron, which formed at Longman on 25th September. The passing on of experience to new units was nothing new for 614 Squadron, it having already contributed personnel from 'B' Flight in October 1939 to form 225 Squadron at Odiham.

Initially under the control of 22 Group, on 5th October 1940 Grangemouth was transferred to 10 (Fighter) Group, RAF Fighter Command. This group had its headquarters at Rudloe Manor in Wiltshire and, on paper, seems a strange choice to control an airfield in southern Scotland. Becoming operational on 8th July 1940, the group was tasked with the defence of Plymouth, the southwest ports, dockyards and Channel convoys and remained in this role until the end of the Second World War. The need for properly trained night-fighter crews within that particular area may have influenced the arrival of the new unit about to be formed at Grangemouth.

Tasked with training night-fighter crews, 58 Operational Training Unit (OTU) was formed at Grangemouth on 21st October 1940. Night Fighter Operational Training was the official description of the fledgling unit which struggled to find its feet at Grangemouth. It relied heavily on the resident 614 Squadron for the most basic of equipment before any of its own aircraft arrived.

As personnel began to arrive for 58 OTU, it was quickly realised that there was an inadequate amount of accommodation on the airfield and several local public and private buildings were requisitioned. These included Charing Cross, Kerse Church, Old Parish Halls, No.6 Albert Avenue and Scottish Oil's Recreation Hall. By 26th October, these buildings were in military hands and, five days later, so was West Quarter School in Polmont. The school was still under construction but, despite this, and because it was situated just three miles from the airfield, it was requisitioned for more accommodation. Further properties were taken over by the end of the year. Sleeping accommodation for officers and WAAFs was requisitioned at Polmont Park, Millfield and Weedings Hall; all around Polmont. Polmont Park and a further private residence were requisitioned for use as the Station Sick Quarters (SSQ).

The first aircraft for 58 OTU arrived at Grangemouth on 2nd November 1940 in the shape of a Miles Master. The following day two more Masters were flown in, followed by a fourth on 13th November; the same day, 150 parachutes were delivered, giving an indication of just how large a training unit was planned.

The main aircraft types that were available at the time and were suitable for night-fighter operations were the Blenheim and Defiant. At this stage, with only five officers and 224 airmen on strength, 58 OTU was contacted by Headquarters Fighter Command (HQFC) and asked when they would be ready to receive Blenheims and Defiants from 20 Maintenance Unit (MU) at Aston Down in Gloucestershire. The station commander and officer commanding 58 OTU at the time, Wg Cdr Hallings-Pott DSO, replied to HQFC stating that the unit would be ready by 12th November. This decision was taken despite the fact that, due to the lack of suitable accommodation, no more personnel were being posted into Grangemouth.

Over the next few days, a plethora of decisions were made about the future of 58 OTU, its role and also whether or not to move it to a more suitable airfield – all just three weeks after its formation. The first decision made was to move control of the OTU from 10 Group to 13 Group, based in Newcastle upon Tyne, on 6th November. Three days later, 13 Group HQ were informed by HQFC that the aircraft and personnel of 58 OTU could not be accepted owing to the lack of facilities at Grangemouth. The following day, senior staff of 13 Group ordered 58 OTU to inspect Perth airfield as a suitable alternative. But Perth was suffering from the same lack of accommodation and the surface of the airfield was not of sufficient firmness to support night-fighter training.

Wg Cdr Hallings-Pott was destined not to see 58 OTU blossom; he was posted to Hawarden in Cheshire on 10th November and replaced by Gp Capt D. V. Carnegie AFC – Grangemouth's first official station commander – the same day.

HQFC instructed 14 MU, based at Carlisle in Cumberland, to commence the delivery of equipment to 58 OTU on 19th November but only two days later, the goalposts were moved again. A decision was made that 58 OTU would not become a night-fighter training unit, but the exact opposite: a day-fighter training unit. The night-fighter training unit would instead be formed at Church Fenton in Yorkshire, becoming 53 OTU on 25th November.

The requirement for 58 OTU now changed to a half-strength establishment of 38 Spitfires, fourteen Fairey Battles and four Masters. From its first formation in October 1940, work began on upgrading Grangemouth airfield with concrete runways and perimeter track. The new runways would be built adjacent to the original pre-war grass runways. An optimistic completion date of 1st December 1940 was given for the opening of the main east-west runway measuring 1,400 yds in length. A second (grass) runway of 1,100 yds was kept open during the construction work for the operation of 614 Squadron and the delivery of aircraft to 58 OTU. The completion date for the main runway proved to be unrealistic; it was not ready for use until 7th February 1941, by which time the subsidiary grass runway was well past its best. In fact, it was in such a state that aircraft were being damaged by the mud being thrown up by the wheels and onto the wing flaps.

As a result of all the changes, 58 OTU was officially formed again on 2nd December 1940, this time as a day-fighter training unit. Without a Spitfire to be seen, the first three officer pupil pilots arrived at Grangemouth on 23rd December, keen to commence No.1 Course on 1st January 1941. A further 24 sergeant pilots joined the officers on the inaugural course.

Experienced instructors were crucial for a unit like 58 OTU and the first of them, Wg Cdr H. A. V. Hogan, arrived from Church Fenton on 26th December. Wg Cdr Hogan took the position of Chief Flying Instructor (CFI) followed by two more instructors posted in from 603 Squadron. Flt Lt Haig and Flg Off Carbury had seen action during the Battle of Britain, both over the south of England and southern Scotland. Their combined experience was to prove invaluable to the trainee fighter pilots.

On the very last day of 1940, four Spitfire Is – the first of many assigned to 58 OTU – were delivered to Grangemouth by Air Transport Auxiliary pilots. The same day, 58 OTU was taken over again, this time by newly formed 81 (Training) Group based at Sealand in Cheshire but destined to move to Tallow Hall in Worcestershire a few weeks later. The group controlled the activities of 54–59 OTUs and would remain in charge until April 1943.

No.1 Course began as planned on New Year's Day with only four Masters and the recently arrived Spitfires on strength. More would follow throughout January, but one was written off on landing by its Polish pilot after colliding with a marked obstacle. While aircraft were obviously in short supply, the pressing need for more flying instructors was also a headache for 58 OTU. Only five were on strength at the start but this number rose to a more healthy nine by the end of January. Basic tools were also an issue; the unit was still scavenging equipment from airfields all over Scotland as well as relying on help from 614 Squadron. It was cautiously suggested, and rightly so, that such basic needs should be met before a unit, such as an OTU, is even formed.

Poor weather also hindered 58 OTU's early flying training but, by 20th January 1941, the first pupil had gone solo in a Spitfire. More aircraft began to arrive and, with the additional flying instructors, the pace began to increase. The fourteen pupils of 2 Course arrived on 3rd February 1941, twelve of whom were New Zealanders. One of the two British pupils was none other than Neville Duke, who would become the famous Hawker test pilot. Duke was commissioned while training at Grangemouth and went on to be posted to 92 Squadron, 73 OTU and 145 Squadron before joining Hawkers in January 1945.

During February, 58 OTU was increased in size from a half-strength to full OTU with an establishment of 68 Spitfires, 22 Masters and six target tugs, the latter consisting of a mix of Battles and Lysanders. The unit was still short of its half-strength establishment at this stage but, by the end of the month, several Spitfires at a time were being delivered on a daily basis.

The list of aircraft involved in minor incidents was already long, but the first of sadly many fatal accidents did not occur until 14th February 1941. Sgt J. T. Silvester was on a training flight in a Spitfire I (L1059) when witnesses saw his aircraft dive into the ground at Hillhead Farm near Slamannan. He had previously been seen circling in poor weather, possibly looking for a place to force-land. Sadly, Sgt Silvester was killed instantly upon impact. The Spitfire I involved in the crash was typical of the aircraft being delivered to 58 OTU at the time. At this stage of the war, all new-production were needed for the use of front-line operational squadrons. As new Marks arrived or aircraft began to

Grangemouth, late 1941/early 1942, with Spitfire Is and Master Is clearly visible. (via A. P. Ferguson)

spend more time on the ground than in the air, they would be passed on to another unit. Arriving on an OTU was usually the last port of call for such an aircraft, indicating that the squadrons had already got the best out of it. Often these aircraft had seen service with three or even four squadrons; and L1059 was no exception, having seen action with 603, 266 and 152 Squadrons before its eventual demise on 58 OTU.

The first of 58 OTU's pupils passed out as Spitfire pilots from No.1 Course on 17th February 1941 having spent a mere six weeks in training. With very few flying hours on type, the fledgling fighter pilots were posted straight to operational squadrons. Their chances of survival increased as each sortie was flown. This was a much-improved situation than that experienced by the fighter pilots of 1939 and early 1940. The establishment of OTUs gave the pupil pilots a much more rounded training course which included more combat training – a far cry from the training undertaken by the pioneering fighter pilots, who often did not fire a single bullet until they were faced by an enemy aircraft.

The first solo flight by a pupil pilot was often more traumatic for the instructor than for the individual in the cockpit. Some instructors would choose to watch their charge like a hawk as he tentatively completed a single circuit, while others would walk away and immerse themselves in a separate task. Whether the two pilots who soloed for the first time on 24th February were under scrutiny is not known. What is known is that their actions would have definitely justified further dual flying training in the Master! The first pilot was about to land when he a struck a pole in an obstructed field and suffered a heavy landing which collapsed the undercarriage. The second pilot overshot his landing and trundled into a Lysander, damaging both aircraft propellers in the process, much to the consternation of the ground engineers.

While 58 OTU continued to grow, 614 Squadron, who had just returned from a detachment at Tangmere in Sussex from where they flew air-sea rescue operations over the English Channel, were getting ready to leave Grangemouth for the final time. On 4th March 1941, the popular squadron, which had helped 58 OTU so much during its early days, made the short flight to Macmerry.

Grangemouth gained another unit on 13th April 1941, with the formation of 4 Aircraft Delivery Flight (ADF), which was responsible for the delivery of fighter-type aircraft to all airfields within 13 and 14 Groups. It only had one permanent aircraft on strength, a de Havilland Dominie I (X7333) that it later lost at Acklington in Northumberland on 8th June 1941 when it hit a hedge on take-off, crash-landed and burst into flames. Luckily, the two crewmen escaped uninjured. The personnel of 4 ADF moved to Turnhouse on 7th January 1942 and continued to deliver fighter aircraft until the unit disbanded at Clifton in Yorkshire in October 1945.

Air Marshal Viscount Trenchard returned to Grangemouth for a second visit on 17th April 1941. He gave an informal address to officers, instructors and airmen at the airfield before continuing with his schedule of visiting just about every operational airfield within the RAF.

Several local landowners offered all pupil pilots serving at 58 OTU the opportunity to fish in their lochs and streams from April 1941 onwards. Permission to play on the local golf course was also obtained for officers, airmen and course pupils. Apparently, both leisure activities were fully taken advantage of.

By May, the size of each course passing through 58 OTU was averaging well over 40 pupils each. With two courses passing through Grangemouth at any one time, a need to reorganise the training programme had arisen. It was decided that more focus should be placed upon Ground and Synthetic Training. This was easily achieved because of the size of the courses and the fact that not every pupil could be in the air at the same time. To achieve this, each course was divided into two flights, rather than the original four. This would effectively result in a whole course being in the air while the other course was involved in ground training. The course still gradually increased in size, however; a typical example being the arrival of 6 Course on 12th May. It was made up of four Britons (RAF), two Poles, seven Australians, eight Rhodesians and 23 Canadians; 44 in total, the largest course since 58 OTU's formation.

More changes took place before the month was out. The four training flights, known simply as 'A' to 'D' Flights, had their establishment reduced to ten Spitfires each. A further nine Spitfires were allocated to the OTU's Target Towing Flight (TTF), all of which were fitted with ciné gun cameras. Camera Gun and Air Firing Practice was to be confined to the senior course only and, on the last day of May, a new range was surveyed in the Pentland Hills, eight miles south-east of Livingston. A site was approved for a new Air to Ground Firing Range on the south-eastern side of the hill range, probably not too far away from the current rifle range.

A second Air to Ground Firing Range was investigated at Carnworth, approximately nine miles east-north-east of Lanark. The range was first inspected for 58 OTU's use in August 1941 but it was not brought into use until a year later. An Air to Air and Air to Sea Range was also used by 58 OTU at Bass Rock, located two miles off the East Lothian coast. By 1942 the Bass Rock range was being heavily used, with one course recording an average of 789 rounds per pupil fired at sea targets and a further 4,530 rounds per pupil fired at the aerial towed targets.

News came on 30th June 1941 that 58 OTU was to get its own satellite airfield, located at Balado Bridge. It was hoped by all at 58 OTU that the weather would be better there than at Grangemouth, whose aircraft were regularly grounded because of poor flying conditions. Accommodation at Grangemouth was reaching breaking point as well and posting several hundred airmen to another airfield would certainly relieve the problem. In July, with over 1,500 officers and airmen on strength, Grangemouth was 360 airmen over its establishment. The following month was even worse: 500 airmen over establishment. Nearby, Avondale House, which was reserved for WAAF accommodation, was taken over by pupil officers and, in turn, the huts that they had occupied were taken over by airmen from the overcrowded Town Hall. Two more houses, Avon Dhu and Avon Hall

71

were used to accommodate several sergeants. The pressure was relieved slightly when 58 OTU's Air Firing Squadron was detached to Macmerry in December 1941, but the problem would not be fully solved until Balado Bridge opened. That day, however, was still three months away.

The WAAFs, who began to arrive at Grangemouth in large numbers from June 1942, were accommodated in three large houses, all located on the southern edge of the airfield. Weedings Hall, Polmont Park and Inchyra Grange were all requisitioned in early August 1942. More buildings were taken over later in the month, firstly Grange School and then 227 Boroughness Road.

Accidents involving 58 OTU Spitfires were regular and sadly very often fatal. To record them all in this chapter would make for very grim reading indeed. October 1941 provides a typical cross-section of what one month's-worth of accidents consisted of. Two pilots were killed when they crashed into hills; two more lost their lives after one failed to recover from a spin, the other from a dive; another pilot was missing presumed killed. There were three heavy landings which caused damage to the aircraft involved, two forced-landings, three taxying incidents, three engine failures and two overshoots. This was seen as a fairly normal month. At the same time, 11 Course set a record of an average of 40 hours 21 minutes flying time achieved in a Spitfire.

Balado Bridge finally opened as Grangemouth's satellite on 20th March 1942, under the command of Flt Lt C. C. O. Stuckey. The plan was for pupil pilots to receive their ground training and the final stages of their flying training under operational conditions at Balado Bridge. The first pupils from 17 Course arrived on 23rd March and it was hoped that more flying hours could be achieved at the new airfield, thanks to its better weather conditions. The movement of personnel from Grangemouth to Balado Bridge eased the accommodation problems at Grangemouth which, by this time, were already improving.

The aircraft establishment of 58 OTU in January 1942 was set at 75 Spitfires, 23 Masters, six target tugs and a single Dominie. The early Spitfire Is were by now being replaced by the more powerful Spitfire II and V, the latter being the most common of all Spitfire models built.

From the start, 58 OTU was lucky in that many of its flying instructors were highly experienced, often with many enemy 'kills' to their credit. In fact, no fewer than 53 of them were credited as aces! Having been posted to 58 OTU after service on a front-line squadron, once their instructor tour was finished, they were usually posted back to an operational squadron. Plt Off D. E. Kingaby DFM was a typical example having gained eighteen victories on his first operational tour as a flight sergeant. He was also the first man in the RAF to receive two Bars to his DFM. Having completed his instructor tour with 58 OTU, Plt Off Kingaby was posted to Debden in Essex on 27th March 1942 and went on to score more 'kills', receive more medals and survive the war.

Flt Lt A. H. Humphrey DFC had been an instructor at Grangemouth since August 1941. He won his DFC for a notable exploit during the night of London's Great Fire Blitz. Flying from Wittering in Huntingdonshire, in a Spitfire, he flew south towards London but failed to encounter any enemy aircraft. Humphrey continued towards the English Channel where he sighted a Heinkel He 111 bomber heading as fast as it could towards the Belgian coast. After a single burst of gunfire, the He 111 blew up over Ostend. Flt Lt Humphrey then spotted a second He 111 taking off from a nearby airfield and promptly shot that one down as well. He was then attacked by a Messerschmitt Bf 110 and, after a short dogfight, managed to damage it but ran out of ammunition before he could finish it off. Flt Lt Humphrey then brought his Spitfire home safely to Wittering. He went on to have a remarkable career, becoming the Chief of Air Staff in 1976 only to pass away from a short illness the following year.

Canadian-born Wg Cdr R. A. Barton was the officer commanding flying training during 1942 with thirteen enemy aircraft to his credit, several of them downed over Malta. At the same time, the Polish Chief Instructor, Wg Cdr M. Mumler shot down at least five enemy aircraft. Rather than suffer being captured by the advancing Russian forces, Mumler flew his damaged fighter to Romania and then made his way through Greece, Morocco and on to England to serve in the Battle of Britain.

In all, 58 OTU created 25 aces of its own. Successes achieved by ex-58 OTU pupils were always reported back to Grangemouth in order to encourage those still in training. The Polish pupils, who were growing in number at Grangemouth, were by now making their presence felt on the operational squadrons. Sgt Szymanski, a Polish pupil pilot who only graduated from 15 Course in March 1942, managed to shoot down two Focke-Wulf Fw 190s on his very first 'Channel Sweep'. By the end of the year, Polish fighter pilots had accounted for over 500 enemy aircraft shot down over Great Britain. Ex-58 OTU pupil Sgt Turek claimed the 497th, 498th and 499th enemy 'kills' in one action on 29th

The Supermarine Spitfire I was the mainstay of 58 OTU during its early months at Grangemouth. Some of these early marks, many of which had seen combat, remained with the OTU until redesignation in October 1943.

December 1942. Two days later Flg Off Langhammer, an ex-58 OTU instructor, claimed the 501st 'kill'.

When the WAAF population at Grangemouth began to increase in June 1942, several tasks originally carried out by men were taken over

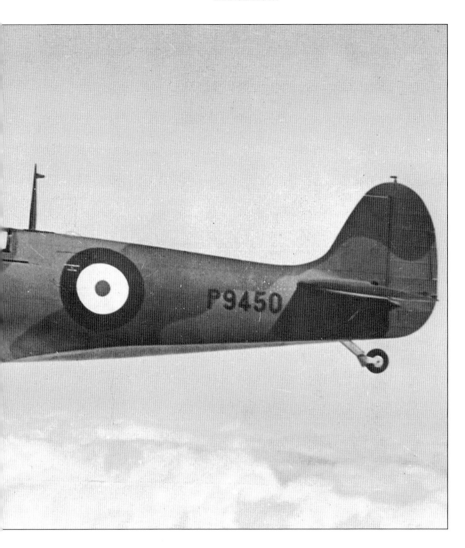

by women. 'Batwomen' quickly took on the duties that had been performed by batmen for the resident officers. The first WAAFs took over the officers' rooms within Station Headquarters (SHQ) and billets at 6–13 Albert Avenue. The vast majority of batwomen were trade-

A group of Polish and one RAF officer pose with a Miles Master as the backdrop at Grangemouth in 1942. By this time all Polish fighter pilots passed through Grangemouth for training before joining a front line squadron. (www.ww2images.com)

trained in the role and the following comment is recorded in the station record book with regard to their effect:

'This innovation at the Station is hardly an encroachment on men's rights, for the women are obviously more fitted for this type of work than the mere male.'

By the end of the year, over 400 WAAFs were working at Grangemouth in a variety of trades including MT drivers, flight mechanics, clerks, equipment assistants physical training instructors, cooks and butchers, aircraft hands, orderlies and code & cypher officers, to name just a few.

Two Canadian pilots suffered the wrath of the RAF disciplinary system on 30th June 1942. Eight days earlier, Sgt J. A. McMillan RCAF and Sgt M. E. Hunt RCAF took the training exercise they were conducting a stage too far. Sgt McMillan was found guilty at a District Court Martial of flying too low near to a railway bridge over the River Tay near Perth; while Sgt Hunt was found guilty of damaging his

Spitfire at the same location after colliding with telegraph wires. Hunt was obviously lucky to have survived this dangerous incident. McMillan was Severely Reprimanded and Hunt was reduced the ranks and given 70 days' detention, all endorsed by the Air Officer Commanding 81 Group. The OTU was losing enough pupil pilots and aircraft in accidents without adding to the number through needless and irresponsible flying.

Extension work on the main runway at Grangemouth began in the summer of 1942 and was completed by September. An additional 80 yds was added at the eastern end and 200 yds at the western end. Despite the increase in length, the Chief Flying Instructor (CFI) Sqn Ldr G. W. Petre dryly commented that the 'Cause of Accident' column in the Accident Diary would still be filled with the entry 'Overshot on Landing'!

When 23 Course passed out from Grangemouth on 10th September 1942, the average flying time per pupil achieved on the Spitfire during the twelve-week course had risen dramatically to over 62 hours. The average had been helped by the addition of Balado Bridge and the 'synthetic city' which had now established itself with a host of ground simulators. The number of pupil pilots continued to rise; and the growing presence of Poles in particular justified the establishment of their own training squadron.

Simply known as 'A' Squadron and divided further into flights, the Polish training unit was under the control of Sqn Ldr Czaykowski and six other Polish instructors. The whole Polish training programme was ultimately under the command of Wg Cdr M. Mulmer, who by October 1942 was the Senior Polish Officer. A promotion to Gp Capt saw him posted to Northolt in Middlesex on 3rd October, his place within 58 OTU being taken by another distinguished Polish pilot, Wg Cdr A. Gabsewicz, who replaced Gp Capt Mulmer the following day. Like his predecessor, Wg Cdr Gabsewicz also held the Virtuti Militari, a DFC, the Polish Cross of Valour (thrice) and the Croix de Guerre. Having seen action in both the Polish and French campaigns, he went on to serve with 607 (County of Durham) Squadron and the Polish-manned 303 (Kosciusko) and 316 (Warsaw) Squadrons. Wg Cdr Gabsewicz had six-and-a-half 'kills' to his credit by the time he arrived on 58 OTU, including a Heinkel and three Fw 190s downed over Great Britain.

By now all Polish pupil fighter pilots would complete their operational flying training at Grangemouth. This effectively made 58 OTU the only unit where British and Polish flying instructors worked in conjunction with each other. In recognition of this, the Inspector of

All these airmen are Polish fighters under training at Grangemouth, Palm Sunday 1942. (www.ww2images.com)

the Polish Air Force presented the 'Honorary Badge of the Polish Pilot' to all senior officers, including Gp Capt C. Walter OBE, the station commander at the time.

A lengthy entry in the station diary looks back at 1942 and gives an idea of what 58 OTU was all about. Part of the entry reads as follows:

'In the course of the last 12 months 400 fighter pilots have "passed out" from Grangemouth – men of many stations, men of varying skill and character, but all imbued with high fighting spirit, trained to the last degree – replacing the gaps in the old established squadrons, forming new squadrons, serving at Home and Overseas. Some have given their lives, some are POWs, others have won renown by their skill and courage. Course succeeds course, the training becomes more intensive...

The primary purpose of the station is the training of fighter pilots, but so diverse and complicated are the pre-requisites for that training that everyone must play his or her part. Health and efficiency, morale and esprit de corps, entertainment and recreation, all receive due attention and thus the station carries on, ready for another year of intensive work and endeavour.'

Regular accidents were commonplace by the beginning of 1943, but to lose three aircraft and two pilots in one incident was tough to bear even for 58 OTU. On 16th January, flying instructor Flg Off H. G Reynolds was leading a section with an American, Sgt D. M. Duda and an Australian, Sgt V. P. Daly as his wingmen. Whilst practising formation flying, the trio was engulfed in mist and crashed into a mountainside in the Ochil Range, near Dollar, approximately twelve miles north-west of Grangemouth. Declared as missing, no more was heard until 1000 hours on 18th January, when a local shepherd reported that he had found a pilot on a hillside. The only survivor of the group was Sgt Daly who had suffered a fractured tibia and various lacerations to his face and body. He was incredibly lucky to have survived what must have been a high-speed crash down the mountainside. The bodies of Sgt Daly's colleagues, both of whom had been killed instantly, were found later that day. Flg Off Reynolds had been posted straight from his 58 OTU course to become an instructor, having already gained operational experience in combat over Malta. He had recently become engaged to a girl from Falkirk.

Poor weather conditions forced a Handley Page Halifax to divert into Grangemouth on 19th February, making it the first four-engined aircraft and by far the largest to land there. It must have looked gigantic when compared to the local Spitfires. As expected, the presence of the bomber generated a lot of interest from both pilots and ground personnel before it left the next day.

Weather conditions were poor throughout the winter months of 1942/43 and continued to be so in the following spring. By the time April arrived, the airfield was in a very sorry state and a great deal of repair work was needed. During the first week of the month, work began on resurfacing the runways and patching up the perimeter track. Additional wire meshing was laid on the grass along the side of each runway to stop aircraft getting bogged down after heavy rain. Ironically, while this work was being carried out the weather was deemed to be too poor for any flying; and on 5th April the rain came down in torrents, complete with a 60 mph gale.

After a major reshuffle of RAF training units, 58 OTU came under new ownership on 15th April 1943. Among the changes was the disbandment of 81 Group, which led to all of the OTUs under its charge being transferred to 9 (Fighter) Group based at Barton Hall, Preston in Lancashire. Formed specifically for the defence of northwest England, its role was steadily changed as the threat to that part of the country eased. The only significant change experienced at Grangemouth was the disbandment of the long-term resident 20 Bomb Disposal Squad (BDS), which had been based at the airfield since May 1941. The squad was responsible for the disposal of all unexploded bombs (UXB) which fell on RAF airfields throughout the greater part of Scotland. This would seem a colossal task, but only on one occasion in August 1941 was the unit called out to deal with a UXB; a 250 kg bomb which fell on Dyce (Aberdeen) airfield. The majority of 20 BDS personnel were posted to the newly formed 5130 BDS Squadron based at Macmerry.

Most units had a resident test pilot, whose main task was to fly aircraft after major servicing or modification. By May 1943, there were two test pilots at Grangemouth, both of whom operated from a small office just outside SHQ. Outside the office a small sign displayed the following:

EADE and SCOTT

TEST PILOTS

YOU MAKE THEM, WE'LL BREAK THEM

W/O A. Eade had been working in this role since arriving at Grangemouth in November 1941. Plt Off A. H. Scott DFM joined W/O Eade in February 1943. Plt Off Scott had seen a great deal of action over Malta and during the regular 'Wings for Victory' campaigns, gave several talks about his experiences to many local audiences.

After Plt Off Scott's departure, one of W/O Eade's tasks was to test the latest modifications which had been carried out in the Grangemouth workshops. All of the remaining Spitfire Is and Vs were being fitted with light bomb-carriers capable of carrying four 10 lb bombs under each wing. Modifications were also carried out at Balado Bridge, and it was from here that the first Spitfire 'bomber' was tested. Another task for the workshop staff was to clip the wings of the early Spitfires, so that they were the same as the shorter, squared-off type fitted to the Spitfire V. Early trials showed that during bombing runs the Spitfire's early elliptical, tapered wing had a tendency to put the aircraft into a spin, usually with fatal consequences.

The year 1943 saw a continuous stream of pilots passing through 58 OTU and, possibly as a result of improvements in the weather, a

The Spitfire V served with 58 OTU, 2 CTW, and finally 2 TEU, all from Grangemouth until the latter disbanded in June 1944.

marked dip in the accident rate. In May the OTU suffered just five accidents, only one of which was fatal and three of which were described as avoidable. In contrast, September 1943 was one of the unit's worst with 16 accidents recorded. Once again though, only one of these was fatal. The OTU had more than achieved all of the objectives set out by RAF Fighter Command, especially during the early months of the war when the need for new fighter pilots was so desperate. In fact, 58 OTU was now producing more pilots than were actually needed; the first time this had happened since its formation in October 1940. With this in mind, 58 OTU was redesignated 2 Combat Training Wing (CTW) on 5th October 1943. The new unit was still equipped with Spitfire Is, IIs and Vs but now with just a few Master IIs in support.

The objective of the new unit was to deliver further training in the art of air warfare to those pilots who had graduated from an OTU. In the beginning, none of the pupils who passed through 2 CTW had any combat experience; but as the unit matured, more advanced training was given to pilots who had already served on front-line squadrons. This would not happen under the CTW; on 15th October 1943 it was renamed again. Now known as 2 Tactical Exercise Unit (TEU), it would become a specialist unit providing operational training for both fighter and fighter-bomber pilots. The Hawker Hurricane I and IV and the Canadian-built Hurricane X all catered for the fighter-bomber requirements. The Spitfire Is, IIs and Vs soldiered on even though they had by now achieved a high number of flying hours. The Master III and Tiger Moth were in support and the Miles Martinet TT.I was used for target-towing duties.

The syllabus offered by 2 TEU took the average fighter pilot's training to a new level. Courses were run for traditional air to air combat, the Martinet TT.Is providing aerial sleeve targets. Various air to ground ranges were used extensively for ground attack exercises, while Balado Bridge still provided a forward operating base centre for synthetic training. One detachment by 2 TEU was carried out from Button Cranswick in Yorkshire from 29th May to 13th June 1944. Twelve days later, 2 TEU was disbanded and both Grangemouth and Balado Bridge fell silent.

Incredibly, after such an intensive period of activity, Grangemouth was reduced to Care and Maintenance on 3rd July 1944, with just a few RAF personnel based there and not a single aircraft to be seen. For over three months, the airfield, despite its earlier vital role was virtually ignored. In early October 1944, signs of life began to return and the empty airfield was placed under the control of 40 (Maintenance) Group based at Andover in Hampshire. On 12th October, Grangemouth was given the unglamorous role of becoming one of 14 MU's many sub-sites. The main unit, which was based at Carlisle in Cumberland, used Grangemouth as an Aircraft Equipment Depot which was destined to remain there until 31st August 1947.

During this time, Turnhouse parented the airfield, until 243 MU showed an interest in using Grangemouth for storage purposes. This particular MU, which was formed at Kirknewton in February 1944 as an Air Ammunition Park, surveyed the airfield with a view of expanding its storage capability. The airfield was found to be suitable for the open storage of ordnance and on 1st November 1944, Grangemouth gained a new parent unit and became a satellite airfield

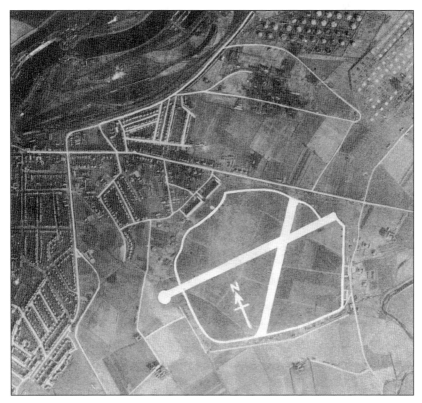

Aerial view of Grangemouth in 1944, with runways and perimeter highlighted in white. By this stage of the airfield's history, the airfield was being prepared as a satellite for 243 MU at Kirknewton. (via A. P. Ferguson)

for Kirknewton. Full control by 243 MU was not achieved until 15th December 1944 and not long afterwards the first of many lorry loads of bombs began arriving for storage around the airfield.

Military flying did return to Grangemouth before the end of the Second World War, but it was a far cry from the glory days of the Spitfire. The new unit was 6 Gliding School (GS), which was formed at Grangemouth in February 1945 with Slingsby I, II and TX.3 gliders. By January 1946 the GS had moved to Turnhouse only to briefly return to Grangemouth in late 1951 to disband. A second glider unit, 2 GS, was formed at Grangemouth on 1st November 1947. This GS flew a diverse collection of aircraft including the Slingsby Falcon III, Cadet I, II and TX.3, Grunau Baby and Sedbergh TX.1 and grew still further when it took over 6 GS's gliders as well.

Grangemouth's most significant post-war flying unit, 13 Reserve Flying School (RFS), was formed here on 1st April 1948. Initially equipped with six de Havilland Tiger Moths and operated by Airwork Limited, 13 RFS later gained examples of the Avro Anson T.I and T.21. A sign of the future brought about the closure of 13 RFS when the local authorities acquired part of the airfield for the expanding Shell oil refinery. The RFS was disbanded on 19th April 1949 and absorbed into 11 RFS based at Scone, Perth.

The last flying unit to arrive at Grangemouth was 4 GS during November 1951. By early 1952, 243 MU no longer needed the airfield and left on 7th January. Not long afterwards, 4 GS was disbanded, leaving 2 GS as the only flying unit left on the airfield. This was one of, if not the biggest glider schools in the country and 2 GS continued a busy existence until its closure was announced in July 1954.

By now, the local council was buying up large sections of the airfield, and if they did not get the land, the expanding oil refinery would. A small regular RAF contingent was stationed here during the final years operating a radio repair centre. The old terminal building was being used by 2 GS when, on 3rd October 1953, this once beautiful building was gutted by fire. By the summer of 1955, 2 GS was winding down and was officially disbanded on 1st September. RAF personnel remained on site until at least 1956, but no official departure date is known.

New housing steadily spread across the airfield from the west, while the oil refinery extended itself from the banks of the Forth south towards the eastern side of the site. Eventually the two met and the airfield was gone. The two original large pre-war hangars remain and in a small open area at Inchyra Park can be seen a small piece of the runway. Having held such promise during the peaceful interwar years, Grangemouth was elevated to the important role of training fighter pilots only to be swept away as if it had never existed. Thankfully though, a small but significant memorial cairn was erected in 1994 in memory of the airfield's wartime role and the sacrifice made by those young pilots.

6
LEUCHARS

With its proud motto of 'Attack and Protect', RAF Leuchars in Fife is rapidly approaching a century-long association with aviation. This remarkable airfield can trace its roots back to 1911 when the Royal Engineers conducted balloon experiments very near to the station's current location. In 1914, whilst en route to Montrose, the Royal Flying Corps' (RFC) earliest aircraft landed near St Andrews to refuel. From its official opening in 1918, Leuchars has been in virtually uninterrupted use ever since and despite harsh military cutbacks it is hoped that the station's future is secure for many years to come. Its squadrons continue to play a crucial role in the defence of the United Kingdom and its territorial waters.

Land clearance for a new aerodrome began in 1916 at Reres Farm, south-east of Leuchars village and on the edge of the River Eden estuary. By 1918 the site was ready for occupation and was placed under the control of 78 Wing based in Dundee. Its first unit arrived from East Fortune on 10th November 1918 in the shape of the Fleet School of Aerial Fighting and Gunnery. A vast array of aircraft descended upon Leuchars including examples of the de Havilland DH4, DH5 and DH9A, Royal Aircraft Factory SE5a, Sopwith Pup and Dolphin and many more. Leuchars was intended to be a Temporary Mobilization Station tasked with the training of aircrew from basic flying through to Fleet co-operation work. The airfield was still expanding when the First World War came to an end, construction work including that of seven Belfast Truss aircraft hangars, four of which still remain in use today. Officially renamed RAF Base Leuchars on 6th March 1920, several RAF squadrons passed through the airfield during the early 1920s.

From 1925 the airfield was known as RAF Training Base Leuchars, which in turn became 1 Flying Training School (FTS) on 1st April 1935.

Superb oblique aerial photograph of Leuchars taken on 28th June 1928. All seven original Belfast Truss hangars are in the centre of the image. (via A. P. Ferguson)

Prior to this, several Fleet Air Arm (FAA) squadrons made Leuchars their temporary home, these including 810 and 811 Squadrons, both of which were equipped with the Blackburn Ripon IIC; 802 Squadron with the Hawker Nimrod I and II and Hawker Osprey; and 822 Squadron with the Fairey IIIF.

August 1938 saw 1 FTS return to Netheravon in Wiltshire, where it had originally formed back in 1919. Leuchars then became a Temporary Armament Training Station hosting many detachments and with a gunnery range now established at nearby Tentsmuir. The airfield retained this armament training role until the start of the Second World War.

Continually developed throughout the late 1920s and early 1930s, by the beginning of the Second World War the layout and extent of coverage of the airfield had swallowed up the original aerodrome. A main runway measuring 2,000 yds in length and a secondary runway (actually 20 yds longer) were built, as was a complex and lengthy perimeter track. Four of the original First World War Belfast Truss hangars remained and were complemented by the addition of four large Type 'Cs', two Bellmans and nine Extra Over Blisters which were constructed before the end of the war. The technical and domestic site, which could accommodate nearly 2,000 personnel, had by now expanded in size up to the very edge of Leuchars village.

The first operational unit to arrive at Leuchars was 224 Squadron from Thornaby in Yorkshire on 20th August 1938. Under the command of Sqn Ldr R. N. Waite the unit operated the twin-engined Avro Anson I, which at the time was being used in its original intended role of general reconnaissance for RAF Coastal Command. Two days later a second operational squadron arrived from Thornaby. This time it was 233 Squadron under the command of Wg Cdr L. G. Le B. Croke and also operating the Anson I in the same role. Both squadrons would take Leuchars into the Second World War but not before they had both re-equipped with the Lockheed Hudson I in May and August 1939 respectively, although 233 Squadron retained several of its Ansons.

Under the command of Gp Capt B. E. Baker DSO, MC, AFC, Leuchars entered the Second World War with its two Hudson-equipped squadrons keen to get into action. The twin-engined Hudson was the first American-built aircraft to serve with the RAF during the Second World War and 224 Squadron was the first unit to receive the type. Operational by the beginning of the war, 233 Squadron was destined to become the second unit to receive this excellent aircraft. The Hudson was a military version of the Lockheed 14 Super Electra airliner and an initial order for 200 aircraft was placed for the RAF in June 1938. This was a controversial decision at the time and was not well received in Great Britain as the majority of people thought that the RAF should be flying aircraft designed and built at home. However, with war looming the decision to acquire the Hudson proved to be a wise one and the twin-engined maritime general reconnaissance aircraft filled a large gap in Coastal Command's operational capability. The Anson, as good an aircraft as it was, only had a range of 790 miles whereas the Hudson could cover up to 1,370 miles and remain airborne for six hours. This was vital for any aircraft operating over the sea and particularly useful in enabling Coastal Command to keep a close eye on, and often the ability to attack, U-boats.

Five Hudson Is were returning from a routine search patrol near Rattray Head when war was declared at 1100 hours on 3rd September 1939. The following day, nine 233 Squadron Hudson Is were on patrol again and it was not long before there was contact with the enemy. Hudson 'T' was attacked by a Dornier Do18 long-range reconnaissance flying boat over the North Sea. This particular Hudson had not been fitted with a dorsal gun turret and so the pilot wisely broke off the engagement. The Hudson was hit several times in the fuselage and fuel tank but still managed to make it safely home to Leuchars. By the end of the day though, 233 Squadron had suffered its first loss, but not as a result of enemy action. After take-off, one of the unit's Hudson Is (N7239) appeared to climb steeply, stalled, turned on its back and spun into the River Eden. The pilot, Flt Lt G. P. Robinson and the only other crewman, Flg Off E. D. Godfrey were killed instantly.

On 5th September, the crew of a 233 Squadron Anson I (K8845) being flown by Plt Off G. J. D. Yorke could not believe their luck when they caught an enemy submarine submerging whilst returning from a patrol over the North Sea. The Anson quickly turned to attack and dropped its entire 360 lb bomb load on the diving submarine. Logging the submarine as damaged the Anson set course for home, but unbeknown to the crew their aircraft had been damaged by shrapnel from the exploding bombs which had punctured the fuel tanks in the wings. Almost back to base, Plt Off Yorke had no choice but to force-land into the River Eden off Shelley Point. All of the crew escaped safely and made it into their dinghy from which they were soon rescued; not long after they were returned to Leuchars to much celebration in the Officers' Mess. It was in the middle of the party that the crew were informed by the Admiralty that the submarine they had attacked was in fact HMS *Seahorse*, but luckily their bomb load did not cause too much damage. Sadly, HMS *Seahorse* was lost in the North Sea in January 1940 and 224 Squadron Hudsons were destined to take part in the fruitless search for her.

On the same day as 233 Squadron's mistaken attack, Hudsons of 224 Squadron were on patrol again and several crews reported seeing Do 18s flying their own reconnaissance sorties. Hudson 'L' reported seeing a Do18 but was unable to attack because frustratingly the Hudson's twin 0.303 fixed forward guns had jammed. Hudson 'O' also made contact with a Do 18 and the pilot closed in from the rear and attacked until his aircraft's guns had exhausted their ammunition. After breaking off the attack the enemy aircraft's rear gunner fired a burst which damaged the rudder of the Hudson, but it managed to return home safely. This action was officially credited as representing the first time that a Coastal Command aircraft had attacked an enemy aircraft during the Second World War.

It was not long before 224 Squadron suffered its first loss of the war when one of its Hudson Is (N7247) piloted by Flg Off H. D. Green failed to return on 7th September. Whilst on a search patrol operation the Hudson was seen to crash into the sea, four miles north-north-east of the North Carr Light Vessel. The Broughty Ferry lifeboat, High Speed Launch (HSL) 104 and Ansons from 233 Squadron carried out an extensive search but sadly found no trace of the crew of four.

A 233 Squadron Anson on an anti-submarine patrol was in action again the same day, but on this occasion it appears that the enemy was attacked. Anson 'L' spotted the enemy submarine just below the surface and attacked with two 20 lb and two 100 lb bombs but no signs of damage could be recorded. The following day, eight Ansons of 233 Squadron began the first of many regular detachments to Montrose to continue escort duties, search patrols and anti-submarine operations.

Despite daily patrols by multiple aircraft, it was not until 19th September that a Hudson of 224 Squadron encountered the enemy. Three aircraft were detailed to carry out search duties off St Abbs Head when 'L' of this group spotted a Blohm und Voss-type flying boat. It is most likely that the aircraft was a Bv 138 triple-engined long-range reconnaissance flying boat which was operated by the Luftwaffe throughout the Baltic, North Atlantic and Arctic specifically looking for Allied convoys. Hudson 'L' attacked the flying boat but the experienced German pilot was easily able to turn within the Hudson's turning circle, making it impossible for the 233 Squadron pilot to attack with his aircraft's twin forward guns. Once again, if a rear turret had been fitted to this particular Hudson the outcome may have been different, but both aircraft went their separate ways without a shot being fired.

While seven Hudsons of 224 Squadron were flying a chain patrol and the first of many offensive patrols, a single 233 Squadron Anson was detailed to find an Allied submarine. The Polish submarine *Wilk* (Wolf), under the command of Cdr Borys Karnicki was the one of five such vessels which had stayed behind to defend the Polish coastline against German attacks. Exhausted of ammunition and low on fuel the *Wilk* was making a dash for England, rather than docking at a continental port and risking internment for the remainder of the war. The Anson successfully made contact with the *Wilk* and she arrived safely in a British port later that day. The *Wilk* continued to fight for the Allies and survived the war.

It was not long before Leuchars-based aircraft were probing deeper towards the enemy with more offensive patrols. On 25th September, three 224 Sqn Hudsons were detailed to patrol along the limits of Danish waters where more Bv 138s were encountered. All three aircraft reported attacking the flying boats: 'L' fired over 500 rounds, 'S' attacked with 300 rounds and 'U' also attacked with a further 320 rounds. While there were no RAF casualties, none of the 1,120 rounds fired managed to bring down any of the sturdily-built Bv 138s.

The following day, 224 Squadron was again in action at a time when enemy activity was on the increase. Hudson 'A' attacked a Do 18, firing over 500 rounds and estimated hitting the flying boat at least 100 times. The Hudson's crew lost sight of the Dornier but believed that the enemy aircraft had been disabled, but a confirmed 'kill' could not be given to the crew. However, the same day a Do 18 was reported to be down on the water and was captured by an Allied destroyer which took the flying boat under tow to the mainland. Hudson 'O' attacked a submarine with three 100 lb bombs but once again no damage was observed. Nevertheless, 224 Squadron was certainly making its presence felt to the enemy over the North Sea.

Hudson 'X' of 224 Squadron came very close to bringing another Do 18 down on 29th September. All four Hudsons on patrol that day reported Do 18 activity but only 'X' managed to get close enough to attack one. The pilot of 'X' fired over 500 rounds at the flying boat, disabling its air gunner who was seen to be slumped in his turret. Hudson 'X' was one of the aircraft that had been fitted with a rear dorsal turret armed with twin 0.303 guns, which obviously made a

A Hudson I of 233 Squadron on patrol over the North Sea during the first few weeks of the Second World War.

difference in this attack. However, owing to the Hudson's position during the action, the pilot thought that the enemy aircraft had damaged his aircraft's controls. Crucially for the Do 18 and its crew, the pilot of 'X' decided to break off the attack and both aircraft parted company. On return to Leuchars it was found that 'X' had in fact suffered no damage.

During the early months of the war, large forces of enemy warships had few worries about moving from port to port and patrolling deep into British territorial waters. The German capital ships were a threat to Allied shipping from the start and keeping an eye on these vessels took up a great deal of Coastal Command's resources. On 8th October, the Admiralty reported several large vessels on the move within range of the Leuchars-based squadrons. Accordingly, six Hudsons of 224 Squadron and three from 233 Squadron were despatched that day on special reconnaissance operations and various patrols. Hudson 'V' of 233 Squadron was the first aircraft of the day to spot and shadow a large force of enemy warships consisting of at least one large battleship, three cruisers and a destroyer. Several of the warships opened fire on the Hudson which retired to a safe distance to shadow the force.

Hudson 'A' of 224 Squadron was the next to encounter the force and accurately described the fleet as being comprised of a Scharnhorst class battleship of 26,000 tons, at least one Königsberg class cruiser at 6,000 tons and a Maass class destroyer; the latter was later increased to five destroyers. Hudson 'A' shadowed the fleet for nearly three hours during which time it was subjected to anti-aircraft fire from the warships and at least one attempted attack by a Bv 138. Meanwhile, three of the other Hudsons continued with their special reconnaissance which developed into an offensive patrol. The aircraft in question were 'G', 'M' and 'U', all of 224 Squadron, and all reported attacking a Do 18 whilst on an Offensive Patrol over Jutland. The flying boat was shot down into the sea, its demise marking 224 Squadron's first 'kill' after a month of trying. Two of the Hudsons received slight damage from return fire but this success raised the spirits of all on the squadron and at Leuchars as a whole. Very little is made of this engagement in 224 Squadron's Operational Record Book, but this was actually the first enemy aircraft to be shot down by the RAF during the Second World War. Credit for the kill was given to Flt Lt A. L. Womersley in Hudson I N7217.

A flight of Anson Is of 269 Squadron began a long detachment from Wick on 10th October. Mainly employed on convoy escort duties, 269

Squadron was destined to re-equip with Hudson Is and more offensive roles would develop. While the common impression of convoy escort duties was that they were quite mundane, they were essential operations to protect the vital logistical support that ships provided.

On 17th October, a pair of 269 Squadron Ansons was detailed to escort a naval convoy, in particular the 6th Submarine Flotilla depot ship HMS *Titania*. The Ansons spent many hours searching for the vessel only to return home without finding it. On landing they were told that the ship had not even left the harbour – not an uncommon situation but a frustrating one nonetheless for the aircrews involved. The same day, Anson 'S' of 269 Squadron was fired on by naval units in the Firth of Forth. Only after lowering its undercarriage and firing a signal cartridge did the anti-aircraft fire cease. I'm sure a toast to the Royal Navy was made that evening.

Both 269 and 224 Squadrons carried out bombing attacks on enemy submarines over the next few days. The closest to a result came on 20th October when Hudson 'L' of 224 Squadron dropped five 100 lb anti-submarine bombs on a submerging enemy submarine. There was a collosal underwater explosion and large quantity of oil was seen after the bomb burst; but despite high hopes of potentially having disabled a U-boat, no loss was ever reported on that day by the German Navy. On 22nd October, 612 (County of Aberdeen) Squadron sent a flight of Anson Is from Wick to Leuchars, the aircraft involved being equipped to carry out more anti-submarine duties.

Only two days later, 612 Squadron aircrews and their 269 Squadron colleagues were in action, four of their Ansons having been detailed to provide an escort for Convoy FN.25 and FS.26. Anson 'G', which was in fact crewed by 612 Squadron personnel, reported sighting a pair of obsolete Heinkel He 45C biplanes. First flown in 1932, the He 45 had perfomed well for the Luftwaffe as a reconnaissance aircraft during the Spanish Civil War; but by the beginning of the Second World War less than two dozen of the type remained in service, making this contact with two of the type an extremely rare one. Anson 'G' made a single pass at the two biplanes and opened up with the 0.303 gun mounted in its dorsal turret, but no hits were observed and the two German aircraft scurried for home.

Before the end of October, both 233 and 244 Squadrons' Hudsons had carried out three more attacks on enemy submarines, all without success. Encounters with enemy aircraft were on the increase and on 30th October both squadrons were involved in aerial battles. Hudson 'P' of 224 Squadron reported a Heinkel off the Earn Islands which proceeded to attack the Hudson. After a lengthy running battle during which many rounds of ammunition were exchanged, both aircraft left the scene without damage or casualties. The same day, Hudson 'L' of 233 Squadron intercepted a Do 18 and made five separate attacks, four with the forward guns and a fifth using the aircraft's turret guns. Over 900 rounds were fired at the Dornier which stubbornly refused to be shot down before the action was broken off.

A Bristol Blenheim Flight was formed as part of 233 Squadron on 29th October, thus increasing the unit's operational capabilties. The six Blenheim IVs were to be used on offensive patrols specifically to intercept enemy reconnaissance aircraft.

Whilst on patrol off the Norwegian coast on 10th November, Hudson 'V' of 233 Squadron encountered a submarine which had intercepted a Norwegian merchant ship loaded with timber. The Hudson was at 7,000 ft when it spotted the submarine, which duly fired two signal cartridges displaying various stars which were not the colours of the day. When the Hudson did not reply the submarine immediately got under way and began to submerge approximately a quarter of a mile away from the stationary merchant ship. Four minutes after spotting the submarine, Hudson 'V' attacked with a single two-second delay bomb, the intention being to keep the submarine submerged while the merchant ship made good its escape. Despite remaining over the Norwegian ship for more than 30 minutes, it still had not got under way before the Hudson had to head home to Leuchars.

Two days later it was 224 Squadron's turn to encounter an enemy submarine. Whilst returning from a patrol in the Lister area, Hudson 'L' spotted a submarine from 2,000 ft and unhesitatingly turned to attack across the vessel's beam. The submarine immediately crash-dived and 'L', now only a quarter of a mile away and down to an altitude of just 500 ft, released a stick of three 100 lb anti-submarine bombs. The navigator carefully watched them fall towards the submarine, which had just submerged, but its dark hull could still be seen in heavy seas. The first bomb exploded directly in front of the conning tower followed by two more explosions either side of it. Air bubbles were seen rising to the surface but by the time the Hudson had circled for a second look there was no trace of the submarine. After a fifteen-minute search, 'L' set course for home. Despite no U-boats being recorded lost that day, it is highly likely that this particular U-boat was damaged as a result of the attack. It was only a matter of time before a U-boat would be sunk by a Leuchars-based aircraft.

Hunting for large German warships was on the agenda again throughout November 1939. The pocket battleship *Deutschland* (later renamed *Lützow* to avoid the possibility of a ship bearing the name of the Fatherland being lost), which was known to be on the move across the North Sea at the time, was the first to receive the attentions of the Leuchars squadrons, several patrols being flown by Hudsons of 224 Squadron in an attempt to intercept the warship.

Another German vessel on the target list was the ocean liner *Bremen*, which had left New York Harbour on 1st September and was heading to Bremerhaven via Murmansk in an attempt to avoid Allied cruisers and submarines. Hudsons of 224 Squadron attempted to intercept the liner as it passed down the Norwegian coast but like the *Deutschland*, it slipped through the net. Later converted into a troop ship for Operation '*Seelöwe*' (Sea Lion), the *Bremen* played no significant role in the war and remained berthed at Bremerhaven until destroyed by fire on 18th March 1945.

Visiting aircraft were common at all military airfields and Leuchars was no exception. In particular, aircraft making landfall after a long and difficult flight across the North Sea would find sanctuary at the Fife airfield. Not all landed safely. Blenheim I L8691 of 141 Squadron based at Grangemouth attempted to land at Leuchars on 1st December, but sadly the twin-engined night-fighter crashed into an adjacent field whilst in low cloud and burst into flames. Plt Off R. M. Williams and three other aircrew onboard were killed instantly. The heat from the burning wreckage was so intense that it prevented rescue workers from getting close enough to douse the fire. On 7th December, Spitfire I K9958 flown by Plt Off D. F. B. Sheen from 72 Squadron at Drem also made an unscheduled arrival. With bullet holes in the petrol tank and having been wounded in the thigh and with a grazed ear after engaging in combat with a Heinkel He 111 bomber off the coast near Montrose, Sheen had no choice but to force-land at Leuchars.

December 1939 was relatively uneventful for the Leuchars-based squadrons, their staple operational flying activity being a series of daily patrols. There was not a single day in the month when at least ten aircraft were not airborne during the daylight hours over the North Sea. These patrols were extended to night time from January 1940 onwards, especially when the moon was bright.

Whilst on patrol on 10th January, Hudson 'A' of 233 Squadron spotted an He 111 flying a steady course towards the Scottish coast. The Hudson quickly attacked from behind, but this initially appeared to do little damage to the enemy bomber. On the second attempt, the

He 111's undercarriage dropped slightly and the rear gunner was silenced, obviously indicating that the Hudson's 0.303 guns' rounds were now finding their target. Once the Hudson's two forward guns had exhausted their ammunition supply, the pilot climbed to 100 ft above the He 111 and dropped two 250 lb bombs in an audacious attempt to knock the bomber out of the sky. The 'bombing' only just failed to work as the two bombs missed the Heinkel by only a few feet. The Hudson continued to attack by means of a 0.303 beam gun and the two 0.303 guns in its dorsal turret before the turret's guns jammed and the action had to be called off. The Heinkel would have done well to make it home but for the Hudson only a claim of 'damaged' could be credited.

Three unidentified destroyers were reported by Hudsons 'R' and 'S' of 224 Squadron on 11th January near Horns Reef. Tragically, a third Hudson I (N7262/'W') being flown by Plt Off A. Barclay was to discover that the unidentified ships belonged to the German Navy's 4th Zerstörer Flotilla. The Hudson was duly shot down by the enemy ships, all four of its crew being killed.

The crew of another Hudson I (N7245) were incredibly lucky to escape unhurt after the aircraft crashed on take-off on 15th January 1940. The pilot, Flg Off A. H. MacLaren DFC, raised the undercarriage prematurely, after which the bomber stalled and slumped back down to earth before skidding across the airfield. The Hudson's progress was abruptly halted by some trees and an electricity transformer before catching fire. The crew of four all quickly escaped via the cabin door as the fire intensified. Approximately four minutes later, the two 250 lb anti-submarine bombs onboard exploded, shattering the aircraft into millions of fragments; only the engines remained as recognisable components.

The remainder of January 1940 proved to be quiet with regard to contact with the enemy. February proved more eventful, however, beginning with an unsuccessful attempt by Hudson 'H' of 233 Squadron to bomb a U-boat on the second of the month. A week later, another 233 Squadron Hudson, this time acting in co-operation with the Royal Navy destroyers HMS *Gallant* and HMS *Borneo*, closed in on an enemy submarine. The U-boat got away, but the same day Hudson 'R' of 224 Squadron intercepted an He 111 whilst returning from a patrol. The enemy bomber managed to escape into the clouds, leaving 'R' to be fired on several times by trawlers from its own side! Luckily, the trawlers stopped firing when the Hudson gave the correct recognition signal of the day to them.

On 10th February, 224 Squadron were in action again when Hudsons 'A' and 'J' spotted an He 111 heading for the convoy they were shadowing whilst on convoy patrol. Each Hudson carried out two attacks on the bomber before it slipped into cloud at only 1,500 ft. In the brief exchange of fire that took place, both Hudsons were hit six times, one of the rounds inflicting a flesh wound to the back of the wireless operater of 'J'.

Two more U-boats were attacked during February, the first by Hudson 'R' of 224 Squadron on the 12th followed by a combined effort by Hudsons 'H' and 'G' of 233 Squadron on the 21st. The latter attack, which was joined by a Royal Navy destroyer, was probably the more effective of the two, but poor weather conditions saved the U-boat which managed to escape. A Hudson from 224 Squadron along with another from 220 Squadron at Thornaby successfully intercepted the German prison ship *Altmark* on 16th February. HMS *Cossack* later secured the release of 299 prisoners aboard the *Altmark*, many of whom were merchant seamen.

The Hawker Hurricane I made a brief appearance at Leuchars when 605 (County of Warwick) Squadron arrived from Tangmere in Sussex on 11th February. The squadron was under the command of Sqn Ldr G. V. Perry and it is quite possible that they conducted a few defensive patrols while based at Leuchars, but it moved further north on 28th February, leaving for Wick.

Another close encounter with a U-boat occurred on 7th March when Hudson 'G' of 224 Squadron bombed an oil streak indicating that an enemy submarine was not far away. A single bomb was dropped on the first pass (another would not release), followed by a second pass on which another two bombs were dropped. Despite the combined efforts of an Anson which joined the attack and a pair of destroyers, which dropped a large pattern of depth charges, the U-boat was not sunk. One week later, Hudson 'T' of 224 Squadron spotted a U-boat on the surface at a distance of five miles. As the submarine dived, the Hudson dropped three bombs 'in salvo', all of which fell together within 45 ft amidships on the port side of the U-boat. A brownish patch ten yards in diameter was left on the surface directly over where the submarine had submerged. Once again, however, it was a narrow escape for the U-boat, which slipped silently away beneath the waves.

More success was achieved against enemy aircraft on 28th March when Hudson 'M' of 224 Squadron, being flown by Flg Off J. P. Stracey-Smyth, spotted a pair of Do 18s whilst on patrol. The Hudson attacked the nearest of the two flying boats six times before forcing it down to just 20 ft above the waves. With smoke and oil trailing from one of its two Junkers Jumo engines, it was judged very unlikely that the aircraft would make it back to its home base. The Hudson's rear gunner, LAC A. H. Webster, also attacked the second Dornier. By this time though, the Hudson was also taking hits and when its port engine was put out of action, the engagement came to an end and the aircraft limped back to Leuchars. Encounters with enemy aircraft continued into April; on the 9th, Hudsons from 224 and 233 Squadrons claimed to have attacked several Heinkel He 115 twin-engined floatplanes and an He 111. At least one of the He 115s was shot down.

From the very early days of the Second World War, Leuchars-based aircraft were in a good position to carry the fight to the enemy. As the war progressed, more shipping targets were being selected within Norwegian ports and fjords. Land targets such as the ports themselves, military targets and airfields were also within easy reach of all of the RAF's bombers. The German merchant vessel *Theseus* was singled out for bombing whilst it was at anchor in Bergen Fjord on 11th April. Hudson 'X' of 224 Squadron spotted the vessel and despite being simultaneously attacked by a Do 18, managed to drop three bombs near the ship. Although these missed the *Theseus*, the decks of the vessel were liberally sprayed with machine-gun fire as the Hudson passed over. The Hudson's crew then focused on dealing with the Do 18 whose guns had wounded the Hudson wireless operator in the elbow, damaged the aircraft's rudder, trimmers and gun turret and inflicted many more hits along the wings and fuselage. By the end of the engagement over 700 rounds had been fired by the Hudson's guns, leaving the German aircraft severely damaged and its rear gunner dead.

During the same operation, Hudson 'U' of 224 Squadron attacked a Do 18 which immediately ditched into the sea, the four crewmen quickly taking to a rubber dinghy. Hudson 'A' of 233 Squadron was also in action the same day against another Do 18. On this occasion though, the return fire from the enemy flying boat was accurate and the Hudson's navigator, Plt Off Evans, was seriously wounded. Despite the pilot breaking off the engagement and heading back to Leuchars as fast as he could, Plt Off Evans died of his injuries before the aircraft landed.

The first of a wave of attacks on the German-held Stavanger airfield on the southern coast of Norway began on 12th April. Several Leuchars-based aircraft took part in a surprise attack but very little damage was done. The following day, two Hudsons from 233

Squadron attacked the airfield again in an attempt to improve on the previous day's effort. The Germans were ready for them and enemy fighters shot down both aircraft before they even reached the target, with the loss of all eight aircrew. A further two Hudsons of 224 Squadron did manage to drop three 250 lb bombs each on the airfield, but the effect of their explosions could not be seen because of cloud cover. Stavanger airfield was proving to be a costly target without any serious impact on its operation.

The Hudsons of 224 Squadron returned to the airfield target once again on 14th April. This time a pair of Messerschmitt Bf 109 fighters accounted for the destruction of yet another Hudson, all four of the aircrew being killed in the process. The following day, Hudsons 'N' and 'Q' from 224 Squadron dropped another six 250 lb bombs on the airfield without any obvious effect.

The importance of Stavanger airfield as a target was highlighted by the arrival at Leuchars of four Armstrong Whitworth Whitley IVs from 10 Squadron based at Dishforth in Yorkshire on 21st April. The bombers had taken off from their home base to bomb the Norwegian airfield and shipping in Oslo Fjord before returning home via Leuchars. The bomber crews reported that two of the Whitleys ('J' and 'G') had each dropped six 250 lb bombs on the centre of the airfield, straddling the runways in the process, and had received a very intensive reply from the many anti-aircraft batteries in the area.

Handley Page Hampden Is of 44 Squadron based at Waddington in Lincolnshire also used Leuchars as a forward operating base to bomb various targets in Norway. The squadron's aircraft first arrived at Leuchars on 26th April, to take part in several bombing raids on Norwegian airfields. The first such raid, on Aalborg on 2nd May, was conducted by six Hampdens, all of which returned safely to Leuchars.

Raids on Stavanger continued into May 1940 and persistence finally paid off during a raid on the 17th of the month. Three Hudsons of 224 Squadron dropped a total of fifteen 250 lb general-purpose bombs and 35 25 lb incendiary bombs on the airfield. Numerous incendiaries fell inside the airfield boundary, starting at least four fires. More incendiaries fell onto the nearby seaplane base and the slipway was also damaged. A single general-purpose bomb demolished at least one hangar, making this the most effective and successful attack on Stavanger airfield so far.

Joint operations with the Hudsons of 220 Squadron based at Thornaby were a regular occurrence throughout 1940. One particular escort patrol, conducted on 24th May, was to prove costly for both 220

Squadron and the Leuchars-based 224 Squadron. Whilst escorting three Royal Navy destroyers, Hudsons 'S' (224 Squadron) and 'N' and 'L' (220 Squadron) came under attack from a pair of Bf 109s. Hudson 'N', its port engine knocked out as a result of the attack, tried to ditch near one of the destroyers, but the pilot lost control at 500 ft and the aircraft plunged into the sea. Hudson 'L' of 220 Squadron failed to return after being attacked by the German fighters; and all four aircrew were lost when Hudson 'S' of 224 Squadron also failed to return to Leuchars. The same day Hudsons 'W', 'Z' and 'P' of 233 Squadron came under sustained attack by another pair of Bf 109s. Twelve attacks were made by the fighters, which damaged both 'P' and 'W' and wounded two of the aircrew. All three Hudsons later landed at Lossiemouth. The callsign 'S' was not a lucky one: another Hudson 'S' of 224 Squadron was lost with Plt Off J. Dunn and his crew on 5th June. It has been suggested that an RAF fighter shot down this aircraft in error.

Amidst all of the action that the squadrons were experiencing on a daily basis whilst flying from Leuchars, 18 Group Communication Flight arrived from Turnhouse on 13th May 1940. This small but important flight is worth mentioning purely because of the fact that it was destined to remain based at Leuchars until November 1959. As with all communication flights, the unit was equipped with a variety of aircraft types, but its actual establishment on arrival at Leuchars was relatively modest: two Percival Proctors, two Miles Magisters, one Supermarine Walrus and one Miles Mentor.

On 15th June, 224 Squadron singled out the ammunition dump at Soma in Norway for an attack. Once again it proved to be a costly exercise in both men and machines, with three of the Hudsons that were despatched failing to return to Leuchars that day. Two were brought down by flak near the target and the third fell to enemy fighters; all twelve aircrew were killed.

Since the evacuation of Dunkirk in late May and early June, the German capital ships *Scharnhorst* and *Gneisenau* had sailed into Norwegian waters. Hunting the two battleships had already occupied a great deal of Royal Navy and RAF resources and would continue to do so for years to come. After sinking the carrier HMS *Glorious* and her escorting destroyers HMS *Ardent* and *Acasta* on 8th June, both ships became priority targets.

On 21st June, two Hudsons each from 224 and 233 Squadrons set out from Leuchars to attack the *Scharnhorst* and its eight supporting destroyers. On sighting the giant ship, each Hudson dropped a pair of

500 lb bombs, but all eight overshot their target by approximately 200 yds. Simultaneously a huge anti-aircraft barrage opened up and once clear of this, the small group of Hudsons came under sustained attack by between 40 and 50 Messerschmitt Bf 110s and Bf 109s. Hudson 'X' piloted by Sqn Ldr D. Y. Feeny was shot down in flames; the remainder, despite being badly mauled, made it back to Leuchars.

Success followed failure the next day when Hudson 'T' of 224 Squadron sank a German merchant vessel after scoring a direct hit with a 250 lb bomb. The same day, Hudsons 'J' and 'N' of 233 Squadron shot down a pair of Do 18Ks. Attacks on enemy merchant ships and convoys protected by destroyers were virtually continuous throughout July 1940, but with little success. By 3rd August, 233 Squadron had moved to Aldergrove in Northern Ireland only to return to Leuchars on 14th September. The Hudsons of 224 Squadron were by now operating in detachments from Abbotsinch, Wick and Aldergrove, leaving 233 Squadron to operate on their own from Leuchars. The squadron was quickly back into a routine of patrols, some offensive in nature while others protected convoys as they traversed the North Sea.

October 1940 was a particularly eventful month for 233 Squadron with several encounters with the enemy. Hudson 'H' spotted an He 115 whilst on patrol on 24th October and immediately attacked with the sun behind it. Less than two hours later, Hudson 'H' spotted another He 115 which casually passed in front at a range of 300 yds and then turned directly towards the Hudson. Both aircraft opened up with their forward guns. Closing rapidly, the Hudson dipped down and under the Heinkel to allow the rear gunner a chance of downing the floatplane. This proved to be a fatal manoeuvre for Sgt Knowles, the rear gunner, who was killed instantly as the Heinkel raked the upper surfaces of the Hudson as it passed underneath. The action probably claimed the life of the He 115's rear gunner as well and after a second brief engagement both aircraft set course for their respective homes.

The following day, Hudsons 'E', 'J' and 'K' of 233 Squadron were tasked to fly an Offensive Patrol along the Norwegian coast. Nothing was sighted and the trio set course for home when a U-boat was spotted on the surface only two miles ahead. Hudson 'E' attacked first and dropped a stick of ten 100 lb anti-submarine bombs from a height of 500 ft, followed by Hudson 'K' which dropped two 250 lb bombs, straddling the U-boat 20 ft either side. During the attack by 'E' the U-boat's deck gun crew opened fire, hitting the aircraft's port engine and puncturing two of the wing fuel tanks, neither of which was full. Other strikes caused damage throughout the cabin and rendered the elevators unusable. Luckily, the trim tabs could still control elevator movement and it was in this condition that 'E' was skillfully landed back at Leuchars without any injuries to the crew. The crew of Hudson 'J' witnessed the first two attacks and subsequently described the U-boat as having been badly damaged and in a sinking condition. The attack by Hudson 'J' failed because at the crucial moment its bombs did not drop. A successful bomb release would have certainly finished off the U-boat which must have managed to escape, because once again no such vessel was recorded as having been lost that day due to enemy action.

A Norwegian Offensive Patrol on 28th October involved Hudsons 'U', 'K' and 'Q' and a violent engagement with three Bf 109s. Whilst using cloud for cover, 'Q' lost formation only moments before the other two Hudsons were attacked by the German fighters. A fifteen-minute dogfight ensued which resulted in two RAF aircrew being seriously wounded before 'U' and 'K' could escape back to Leuchars. As for 'Q', which by now was alone, its crew spotted a merchant vessel in Lister Fjord and commenced to attack it from a height of 5,000 ft. The bombs fell 20 yds away from the vessel. After climbing away, and despite no enemy aircraft or flak being sighted, the Hudson was hit several times by bullets which pierced the wings and fuselage in several places. The pilot managed to coax the Hudson back to Leuchars without any further incident.

Another Offensive Patrol on 31st October yielded a result; but only at the cost of another aircraft and its crew when Hudsons 'U', 'F' and 'R' attacked a group of merchant vessels six miles north of Lister. The merchant vessels were protected by a flak ship and 'F' was the only aircraft to score a direct hit on a vessel; 'R' and 'U' missed their targets altogether. Hudson 'R', being flown by Plt Off W. O. Weaber, was last seen flying over the flak ship after pulling away from its attack. It is possible that a combination of fire from the flak ship and a Bf 109 in the area brought the Hudson down. All four aircrew were killed as a result of this enemy action.

During November 1940, runway extension work at Turnhouse had rendered that airfield unserviceable. The resident unit, 65 Squadron, was moved to Leuchars on 8th November with their Hawker Hurricane Is. The aircraft flew regular defensive patrols from Leuchars during their stay which came to an end on 29th November with a move south to Tangmere. Their place at Leuchars was taken by sixteen Supermarine Spitfire Is of 72 Squadron from Coltishall in Norfolk. The

Spitfires continued the defensive patrols before moving to Acklington in Northumberland, in the process becoming the last RAF fighter squadron to be stationed at Leuchars during the Second World War.

The Hudsons of 233 Squadron left for Aldergrove again on 8th December, but this time they were destined never to return. The Aldergrove detachment of 224 Squadron returned to Leuchars the same day and others scattered across Scotland returned not long thereafter.

The day after the departure of 233 Squadron, a new unit was formed at Leuchars. This was 10 Blind Approach Training Flight, which was equipped with examples of the Vickers Wellington I and IC. These aircraft, as the unit's name suggests, were flown in very low visibility conditions to train crews how to deal with these difficult flying situations. The unit was renamed 1510 Beam Approach Training Flight on 31st October 1941 and by December 1942 began to receive the Airspeed Oxford and Avro Anson. These aircraft were much more suited to this kind of training and were later fitted with Air-Surface Vessel and Beam Approach equipment. Simply renamed 1510 Flight by June 1943, the unit moved to Squires Gate in Lancashire on 15th August 1944.

The New Year started well for 224 Squadron when two merchant vessels were sunk off the Norwegian coast on 4th January. One was a 3,000 ton vessel carrying timber, which after being hit no less than six times by 100 lb bombs, exploded and sunk within a short time. A second vessel of 800 tons was sunk by three direct hits; the force of the resulting explosion rocked the low-flying Hudsons.

Leaflet dropping was also becoming a regular task for 224 Squadron, although targets of opportunity were also on the agenda. Flt Lt Leach in Hudson 'M' on 9th January had just dropped his four bundles of leaflets over Egersund when by the moonlight he spotted a railway bridge that crossed a river. Leach made two attacks on the bridge, both with four 100 lb bombs which clinically removed the middle span, hopefully hindering the progress of any local German forces. As Leach climbed over the town to head for home, several machine guns opened up around the harbour. All were silenced by return fire from the Hudson's gunners.

Another new unit was formed at Leuchars on 23rd January 1941, although this one, despite a name change, still exists today. St Andrews University Air Squadron (UAS) was attached to Leuchars despite being an incredibly busy wartime airfield. The UAS came under the control of 54 Group, with the unit's headquarters being located in St

Andrews University. By May 1944, the unit had gained an Oxford for the loss of a Tiger Moth but two more of the biplanes would return to the squadron by December 1945. The UAS virtually disappeared in early 1946 but was reformed in October of that year, coming under the control of 66 Group. A five-year move to Crail came in 1953, following which the UAS returned to Leuchars in 1958 with the first renaming occurring in 1967. Now known as the St Andrews & Dundee Universities Air Squadron, the unit was re-equipped with de Havilland (Canada) Chipmunk T.10s and the odd Percival Prentice T.1. This situation did not last for long because the squadron was disbanded into East Lowlands UAS based at Turnhouse on 1st January 1969. It was not destined to return to Leuchars until February 1996 when Turnhouse closed. The unit's name changed yet again in 2005 to the East of Scotland UAS and today is equipped with Grob Tutor T.1s.

The Bristol Blenheim was no stranger to Leuchars; a few Mk IVs had operated alongside the Hudsons of 233 Squadron in late 1939 and early 1940. The first of many fully equipped Blenheim squadrons arrived at Leuchars on 2nd February 1941. The unit was 86 Squadron, which arrived from Gosport in Hampshire with its Blenheim IVs only to head south again to Wattisham in Suffolk on 3rd March.

The Hudsons of 224 Squadrons were in the thick of the action again throughout February 1941. Six Hudsons successfully attacked the dockyard and shipping at Kristiansand without loss, although every aircraft was damaged by an intensive flak barrage. Flt Lt Leach was in action again on 17th February when he encountered two Bf 110s whilst flying Hudson 'Y'. The Hudson responded with all guns blazing but during the first minute of engagement Leach was hit in the shoulder by a bullet. He carried on piloting the aircraft for another fifteen minutes before managing to escape into cloud, shaking the two enemy fighters off. As the adrenalin subsided and the pain began to increase, Leach handed the controls over to his navigator, Plt Off Flowers. The Hudson had taken hits in the starboard rudder, turret and fuselage and the trimming gear was out of action. Despite this, Leach and Flowers successfully got the damaged Hudson home without any further incident.

The commanding officer of 224 Squadron, Wg Cdr R. Neville-Clarke, along with several others including two officers from 233 Squadron, were awarded the DFC at Leuchars on 22nd February 1941. Tragically, Wg Cdr Neville-Clarke DFC was killed along with four aircrew when his Hudson I (N7235) crashed near Loch Bradan, two miles west of Craigmalloch just nine days later on 3rd March.

Considering the amount of operational sorties these aircrew had flown, it was particularly unfair that their lives should have been taken on a routine training flight to Aldergrove. Only two days later, 18 Group as a whole suffered a tragic loss. Air Vice-Marshal C. D. Breese CB AFC, AOC 18 Group arrived by air from Donibristle on the morning of 5th March. After only a few minutes on the ground the AOC left Leuchars in a 224 Squadron Hudson I (N7315) piloted by Flt Lt R. N. Selley DFC. It was to be a routine ferry flight to deliver the AOC to Sumburgh in the Shetland Islands. En route the aircraft suffered an engine failure not far from Wick airfield. Flt Lt Selley could not make the airfield and chose a field approximately three-quarters of a mile south-west of Wick to force-land into. Inexplicably, Selley chose to attempt an overshoot but in the process, the Hudson stalled, spun into the ground and burst into flames. All those onboard were killed. Both 224 Squadron and 18 Group as a whole had lost their leaders within 48 hours of each other. On 15th April 1941, 224 Squadron moved to Limavady in Northern Ireland.

Sixteen Bristol Beaufort Is of 42 Squadron arrived at Leuchars from Wick on 1st March 1940. Unlike the Hudson, the Beaufort was capable of carrying a bomb load of up to 2,000 lb or a single 1,605 lb torpedo.

Leuchars, for many crews returning from operations over Norway, often provided sanctuary for battle-damaged aircraft. No. 22 Squadron Beaufort X8935 flown by Sgt Jennings from North Coates, Lincolnshire, just made it into Leuchars on 10th September 1941. The aircraft had sustained 309 bullet holes and seven cannon hits after a fight with two Bf 109s.

Bristol Blenheim IV R3816 of 107 Squadron at Leuchars during April 1941. The aircraft was written off at Manston four months later.

The latter capability obviously proved quite useful against shipping and since the arrival on the squadron of the type back in April 1940, regular success had been achieved. The following day, three Beaufort Is took part in the first of many anti-shipping strikes conducted by the squadron from Leuchars. Two merchant vessels were torpedoed and machine-gunned by the Beauforts.

The Blenheim IV returned to Leuchars on 3rd March with 107 Squadron from Wattisham under the command of Wg Cdr W. E. Cameron. Two days later, four Blenheims went into action on patrol followed by regular attacks on Norwegian coastal targets.

The Beaufort Is of 42 Squadron were quickly making their presence known to the enemy. Whilst on Convoy Patrol on 11th March, a single He 111 attempted to bomb the vessels that the squadron had been tasked with watching over. A ferocious anti-aircraft barrage was fired at the attacking bomber which quickly tried to make its escape. Beaufort 'W' of 42 Squadron had other ideas and shot the bomber down into the sea off Tentsmuir. Three of the bomber's crew were rescued by a naval patrol trawler and landed at Dundee.

Two days later, six Beaufort Is carried out a special sweep of the

Norwegian coast. Several enemy destroyers were spotted and Sqn Ldr A. Hibbard descended to sea level to carry out a torpedo attack on one of the ships. The destroyer received a direct hit in the stern, causing a huge explosion and leaving the ship in an inferno. For this successful attack Sqn Ldr Hibbard was awarded the DFC which along with several other awards was presented by His Majesty King George VI on 3rd April at Leuchars.

Back in October 1940, the Dutch-manned 320 Squadron arrived from Carew Cheriton in Pembrokeshire. Equipped with Fokker T.VIIIw/G twin-engined floatplanes which remained at the squadron's original base at Pembroke Dock in Pembrokeshire and examples of the Anson I, the unit departed for Silloth in Cumberland on detachment not long after arriving at Leuchars. The squadron was in the process of re-equipping with the Hudson I and virtually all of the training was being carried out with 1 (Coastal) OTU. Very little was seen of the unit before it returned to Carew Cheriton on 18th January 1941. By the time the unit returned to Leuchars on 21st March, 320 Squadron also had the Hudson II on strength. The main difference between the two Marks was that the Mk II was fitted with Hamilton Standard Hydromatic propellers, replacing the original two-position type blades and adding a spinner. Now fully operational with its new aircraft, 320 Squadron initially carried out convoy and rescue patrols from 6th April, before it steadily expanded its activities into more offensive duties.

No. 320 Squadron operated the Hudson I and also introduced the Hudson II and V to Leuchars; the latter is represented here.

Having taken part in the first RAF Bomber Command attack of the war on 4th September 1939 against the German fleet, by the time 107 Squadron arrived at Leuchars, they were a highly experienced unit. It was not long before the unit's Blenheim IVs were sinking more enemy ships off the Norwegian coast. On 22nd March 1941, three aircraft, led by Wg Cdr Cameron sighted a merchant vessel of approximately 2,000 tons, at anchor in Egersund Harbour. Blenheim 'M' flown by Wg Cdr W. E. Cameron attacked the vessel from 800 ft, scoring two direct hits, one amidships and the second on the forehold, leaving the vessel burning furiously. All three Blenheims returned to Leuchars safely, although Wg Cdr Cameron's aircraft had gained several holes in its tailplane. Sadly, Wg Cdr Cameron was killed along with two aircrew whilst on Convoy Patrol on 6th April. During the patrol, Cameron descended to 200 ft to formate with an aircraft from Crail. As the Blenheim came alongside the other aircraft, it inexplicably made a steep turn to starboard and slipped into the sea, disappearing almost immediately.

The squadron continued to be busy throughout April 1941 with regular attacks, including an effective bombing of Forus airfield near Stavanger on the 7th. Four Blenheims, led by Sqn Ldr Biggs, destroyed one hangar, machine-gunned several buildings and extinguished at least one of the twelve searchlights positioned around the airfield. Light flak was experienced over the target and all aircraft returned unscathed. Four days later, Sgt Bristow in Blenheim 'U' carried out a successful dive-bombing attack on a 1,500 ton merchant vessel. While a sinking could not be confirmed, the vessel was left very low in the water and several sailors were seen in two small dinghies. The same day, Plt Off Maclaren in Blenheim 'M' caught a U-boat on the surface in poor weather. Four bombs were dropped from 100 ft, but all overshot by 30–40 yds ahead of the submarine. Plt Off Maclaren attacked again, this time using all machine guns available, causing several sailors to jump into the sea from the deck of the U-boat. The submarine retaliated with its deck gun and machine gun and at the same time a pair of Bf 110s began attacking the Blenheim. Air Gunner Sgt King fired over 200 rounds alone at the enemy fighters before Maclaren took avoiding action, disappearing into low cloud and setting course for Leuchars.

The 18th April was not a good day for 107 Squadron, who were in action again with six Blenheim IVs off the Norwegian coast. More merchant vessels were believed sunk, including a 7,000 ton ship by Flt Sgt Walston in Blenheim 'P'. Heavy anti-aircraft fire was put up

A crew of a 42 Squadron Beaufort prepare to leave Leuchars to attack the cruiser Prinz Eugen *on 17th May 1942.*

against the Blenheim which had a large portion of its dorsal turret blown away, seriously injuring Air Gunner Sgt Brown. Sadly, he died a few hours after the Blenheim landed at Wick. Another merchant vessel was hit by bombs dropped by Blenheims 'J' and 'Y' from only 50 ft, leaving it listing badly and sinking rapidly. A third Blenheim IV (R3740/'L') flown by Sgt J. Hickingbotham was carrying out the same attack but his aircraft was seen to hit the water not far from the same merchant vessel which had been hit. All three crew were presumed lost.

Blenheim 'N' being flown by 107 Squadron's newly appointed commanding officer, Wg Cdr A. M. A. Birch, was also taking part in the same convoy attack. It was his first operational sortie since taking over the squadron and sadly it was to be his last. His aircraft (R3873) had already experienced engine problems before leaving Leuchars that day and was late joining the rest of the formation. On return to the airfield an SOS was received, but the aircraft failed to return and was presumed to have crashed into the sea. The following day a search by four aircraft from 220 Squadron, six from 269 Squadron and a destroyer found nothing. The unit's busy time at Leuchars came to an end on 11th May when 107 Squadron moved to Great Massingham in Norfolk.

The morale of 320 Squadron's personnel was raised on 20th April after Flt Lt Elias in Hudson 'K' claimed to have attacked a Dornier Do 17. The alleged enemy aircraft did not return fire and luckily for it, managed to escape into cloud. On landing, it was discovered that the 'Dornier' was in fact a Blenheim from Dyce (Aberdeen); thankfully none of the crew was injured. A week later, Flt Lt Elias in Hudson 'E' was on escort patrol for a convoy west of May Island. Whilst circling around the convoy, Elias descended to investigate a trawler which appeared to be trailing a balloon. Before signals could be exchanged, several machine guns opened up with extremely accurate fire on the Hudson. Several bullets passed through the aircraft, one of which pierced a sea marker causing it to emit clouds of aluminum dust throughout the aircraft, covering the crew. After the marker was jettisoned, Flt Lt Elias decided to continue the patrol but had to return to Leuchars early, because another bullet had punctured the port fuel tank. Within the space of a week, Flt Lt Elias had both delivered and received 'friendly fire'!

Another Blenheim IV unit arrived at Leuchars on 13th May in the shape of 114 Squadron from Thornaby. After suffering heavy losses serving with Bomber Command, the unit was effectively on loan to 18 Group, Coastal Command. Its main role was to provide convoy escorts and anti-submarine and shipping patrols. These long and often uneventful operations were relieved on occasions by attacks on Norwegian targets. These included strikes on Aalborg and Bergen before the unit returned to Bomber Command operations on 19th July 1941 and moved to West Raynham in Norfolk.

Another Beaufort-equipped unit, 489 (RNZAF) Squadron, was formed at Leuchars on 12th August 1941 under the command of Wg Cdr J. A. Brown. The unit was initially equipped with a few Beaufort Is, but these were slow in arriving due to the need for more of the type on operational squadrons. Bombing training was carried out on a dummy ship constructed on the edge of Tentsmuir range and torpedo-dropping was practised against targets set up along the Fife coastline. Operational work-up was slow as aircrew were posted into the new squadron a few at a time. By December 1941, the vast majority of personnel on the unit, as was the intention, were New Zealanders and the squadron was declared operational a few weeks later. By now though, the supply of Beauforts Is had dried up altogether and so to fill

Photo-reconnaissance Spitfires of C Flt, 1 PRU, operated from Leuchars from October 1941. Here a ground crewman removes a Spitfire's oblique camera after a sortie over Norway.

the gap, Blenheim IVs were used from January 1942. The squadron moved to Thorney Island in Hampshire on 8th March 1942 to finally begin operations, but they would return to Leuchars again before the year was out.

Two more second-line units were formed at Leuchars during 1941, the first being dissolved into the second. In October, 18 Group Armament Practice Camp (APC) formed with a handful of Westland Lysander IIs. By 5th November it was redesignated 3 APC within 17 Group. Mainly tasked with target-towing duties, the Lysanders were later replaced by the Miles Martinet TT.I until the unit disbanded at Leuchars on 12th December 1945.

Aircraft from 1 Photographic Reconnaissance Unit (PRU) based at Benson in Oxfordshire began regular photo-recce flights from October 1941. The PRU had six flights scattered across Great Britain, two of them in Scotland: one at Leuchars ('C' Flight) and the other at Wick. 'C'

Flight, like the other flights within the unit, flew a variety of photo-recce Spitfires such as the PR.IV, V, VII and IX. The Spitfires of 'C' Flight were joined at Leuchars by the Mosquito Flight from Wick in December 1941. This flight was also a detachment from 1 PRU and operated examples of the Mosquito PR.I, II, IV and XVI at various times. The Mosquito Flight took full advantage of the 'Wooden Wonder's' range and flew photo-recce sorties deep into Germany. The primary role of both units was to photograph all German military installations, troop positions and shipping throughout Norway. The German Navy in particular was a priority target, especially the battleship *Tirpitz* which was regularly photographed by aircraft operating from Leuchars from January 1942 right up to her demise in late 1944.

The German Navy was a constant threat to the British fleet, especially while it was still able to operate the battleships *Scharnhorst* and *Gneisenau* and the cruiser *Prinz Eugen*, which were about to move up the English Channel from their anchorage in Brest Harbour. The Royal Navy, Coastal Command and Bomber Command were at readiness for the fleet to move and on 12th February 1942, fourteen Beaufort Is of 42 Squadron were sent south to Coltishall. Nine of the aircraft eventually took part in the attacks on the *Scharnhorst* and *Gneisenau* which failed to stop their progress but damaged them sufficiently to keep them in German ports for the remainder of the war. By 17th February all of 42 Squadron's Beauforts were back at Leuchars from where they continued to be more effective at harrying enemy convoys off the Norwegian coast.

On 23rd February, Sqn Ldr Cliff and his crew were returning from an offensive sweep in Beaufort 'M' when an engine failed. Soon it was obvious that Sqn Ldr Cliff would have to ditch the aircraft in the sea and he and the rest of the crew take their chances. The aircraft's wireless operator just managed to send an SOS signal before the aircraft ditched into the sea, but the chance of it actually being received so far from home was remote. The back-up plan was a carrier pigeon, the theory being that a message could be attached to it and hopefully a rescue could be initiated. While the crew were scrambling into their dinghy, the bird, named 'Winkie' escaped before a message could be attached. Morale must have been pretty low as they watched the bird disappear into the distance; the only consolation was that it was heading for Great Britain. Unbeknown to the crew, however, the last signal sent from the aircraft had been received by 18 Group and a search had begun, but unfortunately in the wrong area. Meanwhile the trusty pigeon made landfall and completely exhausted, arrived back at its original civilian home. It was worked out that the crew must be nearer to the British coast than was first thought and the following day, three aircraft of 320 Squadron, three from 489 Squadron and seven from 42 Squadron began a new search. The crew's dinghy was quickly found and by 1400 hours a High Speed Launch was guided to them and they were landed safely at Blyth in Northumberland none the worse for their experience. 'Winkie' was given full credit for the discovery of the crew and was duly awarded the Dickin Medal, named after Maria Dickin, founder of the People's Dispensary for Sick Animals.

Another Beaufort unit, 217 Squadron, arrived on 1st March 1942 from Thorney Island. The unit was equipped with the Beaufort II which was powered by a pair of American-built Pratt & Whitney Twin Wasps developing 1,200 hp each. Very few operations were flown by this squadron, which spent much of its time on detachment at Sumburgh and Skitten. Those that it did fly from Leuchars were costly; two aircraft, including that of the commanding officer, Wg Cdr Boal DFC, were lost with both crews killed. By 7th May the squadron was posted to the Far East, the air echelon being absorbed into 39 Squadron at Malta while the remainder continued on to Minneriya in Ceylon.

A Beaufort II of 217 Squadron which operated from Leuchars between March and May 1942.

113

Having served with Bomber Command since its formation in 1937, 144 Squadron arrived from North Luffenham in Rutland on 17th April 1942, now operating under Coastal Command. The squadron was equipped with 18 Handley Page Hampden Is, an aircraft it was very familiar with having been operating it since March 1939. The squadron spent most of its time at Leuchars training for its new role of torpedo-bombing, which the Hampden's long, thin bomb bay was well suited for. Detachments at Wick in late July and early August, followed by another at Sumburgh in early September 1942, brought the unit up to operational status. On 4th September the squadron was ordered to fly to Northern Russia, from where its main task was to protect the many Arctic convoys passing through the region.

For 320 Squadron, their time at Leuchars began to come to an end from 17th April 1942 when the first of its Hudsons left for Bircham Newton in Norfolk. On several occasions the squadron used Leuchars as a staging airfield during early 1943 for long-range operations from Bircham Newton.

By 21st April the unit had completely moved out of Leuchars, their place being taken on 28th April by another Hampden unit, 455 (RAAF) Squadron, which also had served with Bomber Command and, like 42 Squadron, was involved in the attacks on the *Scharnhorst* and *Gneisenau*. Now serving Coastal Command in the torpedo-bomber role the unit, like 144 Squadron, spent most of its early months at Leuchars training to become operational. However, before the torpedo training began, six Hampdens of 455 Squadron, accompanied by 144 Squadron took part in a strike on the Kristiansand area of Norway on 4th May.

There was no let-up in 42 Squadron's strikes on enemy shipping during May, and on the 17th of the month a second opportunity to attack the cruiser *Prinz Eugen* and put it out of action was presented to the unit. Twelve Beaufort IIs, escorted by ten Bristol Beaufighters of 235, 248 and 404 Squadrons took part in the strike, targeting the cruiser and four supporting destroyers. The submarine HMS *Trident* off Drontheim Fjord seriously damaged the *Prinz Eugen* on 23rd February. Temporary repairs were carried out, including removal of a large section of the damaged stern and the fitting of new rudders which were manually operated by the crew. The plan was then to sail the patched-up cruiser to Kiel were she could be placed in dry dock for more permanent repairs. It was during this voyage that 42 Squadron intercepted the *Prinz Eugen* on 17th May. The Beaufort IIs split into two formations of six aircraft each while the Beaufighters attempted to deal

Some of the aircrew of 144 Squadron pose for a group photograph at Leuchars after their return from Russia in late 1942. (www.ww2images.com)

with over twenty Bf 109s and at least two Bf 110s overhead. At least two of the attacking crews claimed to have hit the cruiser with their torpedoes. The remainder could not confirm one way or another because the anti-aircraft barrage was so intense or because enemy fighters were chasing them.

Virtually all of the Beauforts were hit by enemy fire from the defending ships or the attacking fighters. Three failed to return, including 'Y' flown by the commanding officer, Wg Cdr Williams. One Beaufighter from 235 Squadron had to ditch in the sea on the return leg; the two-man crew, unlike those of 42 Squadron, survived and were later rescued. Despite the two hits claimed, the *Prinz Eugen* continued her journey to Kiel where she was fully repaired, putting back to sea in October. She survived the war and was later used during the atomic tests at Bikini Lagoon in the summer of 1946 before being sunk the following December.

The 42 Squadron crews and their Beauforts had served with great distinction while operating from Leuchars. Aircraft from the unit had also been detached to Wick, Sumburgh, North Coates in Lincolnshire and St Eval in Cornwall during their stay. During early June the squadron received orders that they were to be posted to the Far East and on 18th June, all personnel departed by sea, heading for Ratmalana in India while the Beauforts staged through Luqa in Malta and Shandur in Egypt, joining up with the rest of the squadron in November.

A Hampden TB.1 of 455 Squadron off the Scottish coast during late 1942. The unit remained at Leuchars until April 1944 by which time it had re-equipped with the Beaufighter X.

More Hampden torpedo bombers arrived during August, this time a detachment of seven aircraft from the Canadian-manned 415 (Swordfish) Squadron from Tain which were actually already detached from their home base at Wick. On 10th August the Hampdens were tasked to carry out a shipping strike off the Norwegian coast. All seven aircraft took part, but while en route 'M' with W/O Derinis at the controls was forced to ditch in the sea after suffering an engine failure. Despite the aircraft sinking within approximately 30 seconds of ditching, all four crew managed to escape to their dinghy. The planned shipping strike quickly turned into an air-sea rescue operation during which Hampden 'V' also developed engine trouble, but luckily managed to crash-land on return to Leuchars. W/O Derinis and his crew were later rescued and 415 Squadron went back to Tain a few days later only to return once again to Leuchars on 6th September as part of a full squadron move.

Another detachment from Wick to Leuchars involved 489 Squadron, which returned to the Fife airfield during September and October 1942 from Wick still operating the Hampden I. The unit scored more successes against enemy shipping during one particular attack on 16th September. The formation of four aircraft involved was led by Flg Off Moyniham who scored a direct hit on a merchant vessel anchored in a fjord in south-west Norway. On return to Leuchars he described what happened:

All five ships and the shore batteries opened fire with both light and heavy flak. We dropped our torpedoes and my rear gunner saw the leading ship almost obliterated with spray as the torpedo exploded near its bow. We didn't stay to see any more as there was no cloud and we expected enemy fighters.

All four Hampdens, despite being damaged by flak, returned safely to Leuchars.

By late 1942, photo-recce flights were coming and going from Leuchars virtually on a daily basis. Both 'C' Flight and the Mosquito Flight had grown in size and a decision was made to merge them both into a more established unit. Accordingly, on 19th October, both flights were dissolved into the newly formed 540 Squadron which operated the photo-recce versions of the Spitfire and Mosquito. The latter were mainly tasked with sorties over Norway, but a Mosquito detachment

No stranger to Leuchars, 489 Squadron operated from the airfield on several occasions during the Second World War. A trio of Hampden TB.1s formate for the camera off the Scottish coast.

117

The de Havilland Mosquito PR.IV was operated by the Mosquito Flt and 540 Squadron from Leuchars throughout the Second World War.

was based at Benson for flights over France and Italy. Regular long-range photo-recce flights were also being conducted deep into Germany and over the Polish Baltic ports. Another detachment of 540 Squadron was operating from Gibraltar, photographing southern France and Algeria in readiness for the invasion of North Africa. The squadron returned to its roots on 29th February 1944 when it moved to Benson.

Both 144 and 455 Squadrons flew regular offensive patrols on the same day. One particular patrol on 13th December involved four Hampdens from each squadron. Those of 144 Squadron came across two 4,000 ton merchant vessels plus a few smaller, innocent-looking ships sailing alongside. The vessels turned out to be lethal flak ships and within the space of a few seconds, Hampdens 'R' and 'M' had been shot down into the sea, the crews of each aircraft standing no chance of survival. Hampden 'N' was also damaged by flak but made it back to Leuchars on one engine. Simultaneously, 455 Squadron came across four merchant vessels which seemed to be unescorted. All four Hampdens carried out torpedo attacks, but only 'L' managed to hit a vessel. The aircraft was lucky to survive its own attack; as it swooped over the vessel it had targeted, the torpedo exploded with such a force that the blast flipped the Hampden upside down. The Hampden returned home safely, along with the three other 455 Squadron aircraft.

During January 1943, 144 Squadron flew the majority of its shipping strikes from Sumburgh while 455 Squadron remained at Leuchars. Twelve Hampdens of 455 Squadron left Leuchars for another shipping strike on 11th January, all with high hopes of finding some prey off the Norwegian coast. The sortie proved to be a disaster with no shipping found and two more aircraft lost. Plt Off Hill and his crew in 'P' failed to return and Flt Sgt Watt in 'R' crashed approximately five miles north-east of the airfield, killing Air Gunner Sgt D. Martin. A third aircraft returned home early owing to port engine trouble.

January was not good for 540 Squadron either; their generally good safety record was tarnished with the loss of two Spitfires in as many days. Flg Off Anderson's Spitfire PR.IV (R7041) failed to return from a shipping reconnaissance sortie on 12th January. The following day, W/O Payne went missing in his Spitfire PR.IV (R7044) whilst on a photo-recce sortie to Stadlandet. A thorough search by Hudsons of 279 Squadron based at Thornaby found no trace of the missing aircraft.

During January, 144 Squadron began converting from the Hampden I to the Beaufighter VIC. Powered by two 1,670 hp Bristol Hercules engines, this highly effective fighter-bomber was considerably more suited to Coastal Command's operations. It was capable of carrying up to eight rockets under the wings or a single torpedo under the fuselage, the latter capability earning this variant the nickname 'Torbeau'.

The same month also saw the arrival of another Beaufighter VIC-equipped unit, 235 Squadron from Chivenor in Devon on 21st January. Eight days later, the squadron flew as fighter escort for four Hampdens of 489 Squadron and seven from 455 Squadron. The shipping strike was a great success with 489 Squadron sinking a merchant vessel and 455 Squadron sinking at least two other ships. The presence of the Beaufighters with their four 20 mm nose-mounted cannons certainly helped the Hampden crews to concentrate on the target rather than worrying about enemy fighters, which stayed away from this particular raid.

The following day, 235 Squadron went hunting on their own, coming across a convoy of one merchant vessel of 3,000 tons with at least five armed trawlers of 500 tons each. The Beaufighters for this particular operation were each fitted with a pair of 250 lb bombs, rather than a torpedo. This eventually became a permanent optional fit for the later Mk.X which would become the most effective shipping strike

Serving with 455 and 489 Squadrons from late 1943 to April 1944, the Beaufighter Xs were in great numbers at Leuchars.

Beaufighter variant ever built. On this particular operation, Beaufighter 'M' attacked the merchant vessel, dropping its pair of 250 lb bombs from only 50 ft and simultaneously firing its 20 mm cannon. Owing to low cloud a hit could not be confirmed, although the ship would have not escaped being seriously damaged.

Beaufighter attacks on the enemy ships continued, the 250 lb bombs being used with varying degrees of success. Often the Beaufighters caused just as much damage with their 20 mm cannon, which could accurately pour into the enemy vessel. Sgt Widmore, once again flying in 'M', scored the squadron's first aerial 'kill' on 2nd February when, after spotting a group of vessels at anchor, a Blohm und Voss flying boat was seen flying away towards Hjelte Fjord. Widmore closed to point-blank range behind the enemy aircraft and one quick burst of cannon fire was all that was needed to send the crippled aircraft into the sea. Enemy shore batteries opened up on the Beaufighter, damaging the port aileron, but Widmore managed to make it back safely to Leuchars.

The same day another 235 Squadron Beaufighter encountered a pair of Fw 190s north of Stavanger. Beaufighter 'B' piloted by Sgt Chapman with navigator Sgt Leach, battled with the Luftwaffe fighters for nearly half an hour. The Beaufighter and its crew were struck several times by bullets during the dogfight. Chapman received a severe bullet wound in the shoulder and Leach was hit in the foot. After making good their escape, Sgt Chapman force-landed 'B' at Peterhead and both crew lived to fight another day.

From the beginning of March 1943, 235 Squadron began to detach its aircraft at various airfields. Sumburgh was the site of the first detachment, followed by operations from Tain and St Eval. Some operations were carried out from Leuchars, and by late July the squadron had regrouped at Leuchars only to move to Portreath in Cornwall on 29th August 1943.

By March, 144 Squadron had become fully operational on the Beaufighter VIC, the last of its trusty Hampdens leaving Leuchars the same month. Very few operations were flown from Leuchars before the squadron moved to Tain on 8th April 1943. The squadron moved again the following month, this time to North Africa and it was over the Mediterranean that the squadron made full use of their new Beaufighters.

Originally formed at Woodhaven on 17th February with a Catalina I and IB, 1477 Flight also had a land-based element that was formed at Leuchars on 16th April 1943 with six Mosquito IIs and a pair of Beaufighter VICs it had inherited from 235 Squadron. The Mosquitos were primarily used for shipping reconnaissance work along the Norwegian coast, but being armed they also encountered and often shot down enemy aircraft as well. By 5th May 1943, the unit was redesignated 333 Squadron with 'A' Flt at Woodhaven and 'B' operating from Leuchars.

By September 1943, 333 Squadron began to receive examples of the Mosquito VI, the older Mk IIs leaving the unit the same month. Several Mosquitos failed to return to Leuchars during late 1943 but on 21st January 1944, the squadron scored its first enemy 'kill'. The Mosquito VI involved was 'K' flown by Sub Lt Jensen with his navigator, Plt Off Thorkildsen and their victim was a Bv 138 which they spotted during a shipping reconnaissance sortie. Jensen dived to 200 ft above the sea and at a range of 500 yds fired one burst which set both of the flying boat's outer engines ablaze. The flames were quickly extinguished by the crew but Jensen attacked again and set the engines on fire for a second time. This time, the fire quickly spread along the whole of the port wing, enveloping the aircraft in flames. Seconds later, the flying boat turned on its back and crashed into the sea without ever firing a shot at its Mosquito attacker.

By the summer of 1944 the Norwegian crews of 333 Squadron were quite prepared to attack anything. One example of this involved Lt J. M. Jacobsen and his navigator, 2nd Lt P. C. Hansen, who were flying a patrol in a Mosquito VI (HP860) late in the evening on 16th June 1944. Leuchars received a garbled message at 2259 hours indicating that the crew was in serious trouble. Only minutes before this message was sent, Hansen had spotted a U-boat on the surface; it turned out to be U-804 commanded by Oblt zur See H. Meyer. Hansen's attack on the U-boat was subsequently described by Meyer as follows:

Grid AN2333, 2359 hours. Attack by two-engined aircraft. Flak, strafing, hits observed on the aircraft. It crosses over the boat emitting a heavy smoke stream. It disappears into the darkness rapidly losing height. No bombs. Five crewmen wounded on the boat.

Return fire from the U-boat had hit HP860's port engine and split open the leading edge of the wing, forcing Hansen to ditch. This was carried out successfully and both crewmen escaped into their dinghy where they would remain for the next 30 hours. Incredibly, U-1000 commanded by Oblt zur See W. Müller surfaced to investigate the small craft, rescued the two airmen and landed them at Bergen to spend the rest of the war in a POW camp. On 1st September 1944, 'B' Flight of 333 Squadron moved their Mosquito VIs to Banff and then on to Norway in June 1945, from where they were later amalgamated into the Royal Norwegian Air Force.

On 6th October 1943, 489 Squadron returned to Leuchars from Wick whilst in the midst of converting to the Beaufighter X. During the previous year's operations from Scottish bases, the squadron had sunk over 36,000 tons and damaged a further 30,000 tons of shipping; very impressive considering that the Hampdens it used at the time were effectively pre-war bombers. The Beaufighter X, 2,205 of which were built, represented the final production model and virtually all of them were allocated to Coastal Command. The squadron spent the remainder of the year becoming operational on the new type. Another unit to withdraw its Hampdens in favour of Beaufighter Xs was 455 Squadron, which did so by December 1943.

By January 1944, 489 Squadron were declared fully operational and on the 14th of the month, eight Beaufighter Xs set out from Leuchars to patrol The Naze to Egersund. Three of the aircraft ('X', 'Z' and 'O') were each carrying a single 18 in Mk.XV torpedo while the remainder ('L', 'K', 'A', 'N' and 'T') were configured for fighter protection and anti-flak duties. At 1242 hours a convoy was spotted consisting of six vessels, including a single merchant ship weighing in at 5,000 tons plus two minesweepers and two flak trawlers. Flg Off Tonks in 'X' began

The Officer Commanding 455 Squadron, Wg Cdr J. N. Davenport is flanked by OC 'A' Flt, Sqn Ldr A. L. Wiggins (left) and OC 'B' Flt, C. G. Milson. (www.ww2images.com)

the attack on the merchant vessel, dropping his torpedo at a distance of 800 yds; simultaneously his aircraft was struck by flak in the nose but causing no injury to the crew. The torpedo found its target, sending a huge white plume of smoke which quickly turned black from the centre of the vessel. Following close behind Tonks' aircraft, Flg Off Branton in 'Z' and Flt Sgt Tuck in 'O' both dropped their torpedoes towards the merchant vessel. At least one more torpedo struck the ship, causing a huge explosion at the bow; the chances of it remaining afloat for much longer were slim. Meanwhile, the anti-flak Beaufighters attacked the convoy with at least 100 rounds of cannon fire each, hitting vessels several times. All returned safely to Leuchars satisfied that the Beaufighter was ideal for this type of shipping strike. After Flg Off Tonks landed, the flak inflicted during the attack caused the nose of Beaufighter 'X' to fall off!

St Andrews-born, Sqn Ldr Kellow led eight more 489 Squadron Beaufighter Xs on a coastal patrol in the Ergo area on 20th January 1944. A small merchant ship was the first target, but as the attack began

The Beaufighter X could also be modified to carry 250 lb bombs under the fuselage which were very effective when attacking shore targets.

Sqn Ldr Kellow was distracted by smoke on the horizon, which he thought might lead to a bigger target. Leaving the small ship in flames the Beaufighters headed for the smoke which turned out to be an auxiliary minelayer being escorted by a pair of 'M' class minesweepers. Two Beaufighters attacked the minelayer with their torpedoes as it tried desperately to change course to avoid the underwater weapons. The minelayer was struck just aft of amidships, sending a large plume of water into the air, followed by a huge explosion; it sank not long thereafter. During this action, the two minesweepers were attacked by relentless cannon fire from the Beaufighters but still managed to inflict some flak damage on their attackers. All eight aircraft returned safely to Leuchars.

During late February the squadron was tasked with providing air cover for the submarine HMS *Stubborn*. The submarine had been damaged after attacking a German convoy off Folda Fjord and was being towed back to Scotland for repairs. The Beaufighter Xs flew seven patrols, much to the appreciation of the Flag Officer Submarines who signalled to the squadron the following:

I am most grateful for your valuable help in getting Stubborn safely home.

124

The aircrews of 455 Squadron were operational on their new Beaufighters by March 1944, by which time plans for a new ANZAC Wing in Coastal Command were well under way. On 6th March a preliminary operation was conducted from Leuchars involving four 489 Squadron Beaufighter Xs fitted with torpedoes, the aircraft being flown by the New Zealanders. The Australians of 455 Squadron provided fighter protection with a further eight Beaufighter Xs. A vessel of approximately 2,000 tons was sunk during this shipping strike, while the cannon-armed Beaufighters scored numerous hits on other ships. The combination of aircraft was a great success and marked the beginning of a partnership that would last until the end of the war. By mid-April 1944, the ANZAC Wing was established at Langham in Norfolk, 489 Squadron having left Leuchars on 8th April with 455 Squadron following on the 14th. Both squadrons went on to even greater success, causing havoc amongst German shipping attempting to sail along the North Sea coastline. In late October 1944 the ANZAC Wing returned to Scotland, this time to Dallachy.

Aircraft that would become synonymous with the final months of the war at Leuchars began to arrive at the airfield in March 1944. Black-painted USAAF Consolidated B-24 Liberators of the 801st Bomb Squadron, 492nd Bomb Group from Harrington in Northamptonshire were tasked with flying clandestine operations into Norway. Under the command of Col B. Balchen, the unit was nicknamed the 'Carpetbaggers' and their main task whilst operating from Leuchars was to carry out Operation *Ball*. The B-24s were all specially converted to drop agents through what was known as the 'Joe Hole'. The Special Operations Executive agents were known as 'Joes' and they parachuted through an aperture in the floor of the fuselage, where the bomber's ventral turret was normally positioned. Other equipment, stored in canisters and dropped from the bomb bay was also carried. The 'Carpetbagger' B-24s carried out 65 clandestine operations from Leuchars, but only 37 of the drops were successful and seven aircraft were lost in the process.

The 'Carpetbaggers' also took part in Operation *Sonnie* which ferried back ex-internees from Sweden. The B-24s used for this task were in standard military camouflage but each carried a civilian registration. The crews wore airline-style clothing, so as to allow them to fly freely to and from Sweden. *Sonnie* B-24s flew to Bromma airport in Stockholm and were serviced by American engineers living as civilians in the Swedish capital. German agents based in Stockholm constantly surveyed the activities of the personnel involved with the operation.

A Consolidated B-24 Liberator of the 801st/492nd BG on detachment at Leuchars during Operations Ball *and* Sonnie *during 1944.*

The flights were very hazardous and were usually undertaken when cloud cover was available; luckily only one *Sonnie* B-24 was lost when it crashed into a mountain in October 1944. Combined with other aircraft involved in Operation *Sonnie*, a total of 4,304 passengers were flown from Sweden to Leuchars before the war's end.

Since 1941, Sweden had also been the destination of flights operated by Leuchars-based aircraft of the British Overseas Aircraft Corporation (BOAC). Initially operated by Hudsons, from 1943 the Mosquito proved to be the best aircraft for the job, its speed keeping it out of trouble as well as enabling it to make good use of cloud cover to help it evade enemy fighters. The Mosquito obviously could not carry a huge amount of cargo, but mail and even engineering items such as ball-bearings were carried. The bomb bay on several aircraft was also converted to carry a single passenger. By 1945, Douglas Dakotas and Lockheed Lodestars had begun to fly the route as the chances of encountering an enemy fighter began to diminish. Flak was often encountered in the Skaggerak area but since the route began not a single aircraft was lost to enemy fire, although several were lost in accidents. On 17th May 1945, the BOAC service was moved to Northolt in Middlesex, by which time the Mosquitos alone had completed 520 round trips from Leuchars.

More Liberators arrived on 11th July 1944, but this time they were RAF Mk VIs that belonged to 206 Squadron, Coastal Command from St Eval. Based on the B-24H and J, the Liberator VI was the most common of all the RAF's variants, 1,568 examples being built.

It was not long before 206 Squadron claimed its first U-boat destroyed from Leuchars, but sadly it was at the cost of the ten-man crew of one of the unit's Liberator VIs (EV937/'E'). With Flg Off D. W. Thynne at the controls the aircraft took off for a patrol of the Norwegian coast on 15th July. Nothing more was heard from the aircraft and it can only be concluded that it had a fatal encounter with U-319 commanded by Oblt zur See J. Clemens. The U-boat had sailed from Stavanger on 5th July to take up position off the south-west coast of Norway for anti-invasion duties. Another 206 Squadron Liberator VI found wreckage and a single body, which was later identified as being that of Sgt N. Hilton, in a dinghy in the same position. The presumption was that whilst carrying out an attack the Liberator was brought down by fire from the U-boat's deck gun. Shells from the U-boat and depth charges from the Liberator both found their respective targets and destroyed each other virtually simultaneously.

BOAC flew routes into Norway and Sweden from Leuchars between 1941 and 1945. Mosquitos alone flew 520 round trips.

This was not a good time for 206 Squadron, because the following day another of its Liberator VIs (EV947) failed to return from operations, its ten-man crew once again presumed lost. Another of the squadron's aircraft (EV873) crashed at the end of the Leuchars runway on 20th July after an aborted take-off. The Liberator's pilot and co-pilot, Flt Lt Hancock and Plt Off Tulloch RCAF respectively, were killed while the remainder of the crew managed to escape with slight injuries and shock.

Flg Off Carlisle and his crew in Liberator 'S' claimed a second U-boat for the squadron on 28th September 1944. Whilst on patrol, the Liberator attacked an unknown submarine it had caught on the surface with seven depth charges. Flg Off Carlisle banked his aircraft around to attack the submarine with the one remaining depth charge. By now the U-boat was trying to carry out violent evasive manoeuvres before the last depth charge was dropped 50 ft in front of the vessel. The Liberator followed up with several more passes, pouring fire from its front and mid-upper turrets into the U-boat, leaving it trailing an oil slick a mile long and 200 yds wide. Approximately twenty single-man dinghies were seen, most of them occupied and behind the submarine. No U-boat loss is officially recorded for 19th September, but it is quite possible that at best, if it made back to a friendly port, it probably never sailed again. It is also possible that it may have sunk before getting that far.

A second Liberator VI-equipped unit arrived at Leuchars on 28th September 1944 in the shape of 547 (Kingfisher) Squadron, also from St Eval, and under the command of Wg Cdr McKenzie. Two days later, three of the squadron's aircraft flew their first patrols from Leuchars and by 12th October the squadron saw their first action when Liberator 'G' spotted a U-boat on the surface in poor weather. The submarine manoeuvred quickly, causing the Liberator to overshoot its target but allowing the gunners in the mid-upper and tail turrets to fire several rounds at the vessel before losing sight of it.

The squadron lost its first aircraft whilst serving at Leuchars on 17th October 1944. Liberator 'S' was returning from a patrol when at 2125 hours it crashed into Wirren Hill, five and half miles north-west of Edzell. Seven of the crew were killed outright, but luckily four survived although all were injured. Ten days later, Flg Off P. F. Lewcock and his ten crewmen were lost without trace whilst on patrol off Norway.

Encounters with enemy aircraft continued when Liberator 'D' of 206 Squadron piloted by Flg Off M. J. Frost came under relentless attack on

Both 206 and 547 Squadrons operated the Liberator VI from July 1944 to the end of the war.

15th November. Three Bf 110s positioned themselves behind the aircraft and attacked it at least nine times. The tail gunner was wounded very early on in the confrontation but continued firing his guns throughout. Untold hits were recorded on the Liberator, some of which killed the port beam gunner. The mid-upper gunner managed to hit one of the Bf 110s in its port engine, causing the pilot to break off his attack with his aircraft in flames. Eventually the bullet-riddled Liberator managed to shake off the fighters and carried out a belly-landing at Sumburgh where the aircraft was later deemed to be beyond economical repair.

Both of the Liberator VI squadrons were equipped with 22-million candle power Leigh Lights which could be fitted to the underside of the Liberator's wing. These incredibly powerful lights could illuminate a vessel on the surface on the darkest of nights. The standard practice was to use the aircraft's ASV radar to gain contact and guide the Liberator towards the target. At the last moment the Leigh Light was turned on, catching the target in its beam for the pilot and bomb-aimer and air gunners to attack. Liberator 'E' of 547 Squadron used this system on 13th February to surprise a U-boat. Six 250 lb depth charges were dropped once the Leigh Light had been switched on and the target illuminated, this also giving the nose turret gunner the opportunity to open fire. Luckily for the submarine, radar contact was lost after the first pass, and it was lucky to escape.

From February 1945, both squadrons began to receive the Liberator VIII. Based on the B-24J, the first example arrived at Leuchars for 206 Squadron on 20th February. By the end of March, both 206 and 547 Squadrons had received this, the definitive Mark which would remain in service until both squadrons' disbandment many months after the war's end.

At least two special operations were organised for 547 Squadron during March 1945. The first, on 23rd March, was led by Wg Cdr McKenzie and involved eight Liberator VIIIs tasked with finding a large enemy convoy off the Norwegian coast. The convoy of over 30 ships, of which some were estimated at over 6,000 tons, was easily found. The Liberators attacked the vessels with a variety of weapons, including depth charges and anti-submarine bombs, leaving many of the ships burning. A U-boat was also attacked by Liberator 'H' with ten 250 lb depth charges and once again was lucky to escape intact. Three days later, eleven Liberator VIIIs of 547 Squadron carried out a similar attack on another convoy that was made up of destroyers, merchant vessels and U-boats. Although no ships were sunk, many were left damaged and with no option but to make for the nearest friendly port for repairs. All of 547 Squadron's aircraft returned to Leuchars safely.

Liberator 'B' of 206 Squadron used its Leigh Light to full effect when it caught a U-boat on the surface on 3rd April. The aircraft dropped four 600 lb anti-submarine bombs and fired over 100 rounds from its front turret. The crew were convinced that the U-boat had been badly damaged at the bow, but frustratingly once again, 206 Squadron could not claim another enemy submarine sunk.

With the war drawing to a close, and U-boats trying to make it back to Germany, more were being sunk by air attacks. Five U-boats were sunk on 5th May, three of them as a result of attacks from the air. One of the vessels was U-579 which was sailing with U-733 and the steamer *Ostwind*. Flg Off A. A. Bruneau DFC in Liberator 'E' of 547 Squadron singled out U-579 and bombed it with several depth charges, sinking the submarine with the loss of 24 hands, including the captain, Schwarzenberg. Liberator 'T' of 206 Squadron attacked a U-boat with six 250 lb depth charges, which straddled the submarine. Despite a large amount of debris and oil no claim could be made.

The day did not go entirely in Coastal Command's favour. Liberator

'E' of 547 Squadron, being flown by Flt Lt G. W. Hill, joined in an attack on U-534 approximately thirteen miles north-east of Anholt in Denmark. A Liberator VIII (KH347) of 86 Squadron was already attacking the U-boat when 'E' arrived, so the gunners on the deck of the U-boat were ready for action. Flt Lt Hills' Liberator VIII took several hits from the submarine's 20 mm and 37 mm flak guns. The fire was accurate enough to rip one of the Liberator's wings off, sending the aircraft crashing into the sea. Only one airman survived, later being spotted by Liberator 'C' from 206 Squadron. The 86 Squadron Liberator, flown by W/O J. D. Nicol DFC continued its attack and eventually sunk U-534 with the loss of three crewmen, while a further 49 were later rescued.

Post-war rumours of Nazi gold aboard U-534 resulted in the submarine being raised to the surface in 1993. No gold was found and the U-boat was moved to the Warship Preservation Trust in 1996. The Trust's museum closed in 2007 and U-534 was acquired by Mersey Travel to be displayed at the Woodside Ferry Terminal. The U-boat has since been cut into four sections in order to reduce transportation costs and will be displayed in section form to allow better access for the general public.

This brings to an end the wartime operations of RAF Leuchars. The most demanding job remaining for 206 and 547 Squadrons was to escort the large number of U-boats and German warships which had surrendered with the ending of the Second World War in Europe on 8th May 1945. The end of this task led to the disbandment of 547 Squadron at Leuchars on 4th June, while 206 Squadron was moved to Oakington in Cambridgeshire on 31st July 1945. It was disbanded in April 1946, reformed as a transport squadron in November 1947 and disbanded again in February 1950. Two years later it was reformed yet again and equipped with the Avro Shackleton MR.1A, MR.2 and MR.3 for maritime patrol duties. The Shackletons were replaced in turn by the Hawker Siddeley Nimrod MR.1 in 1970; a type which the squadron continued to operate in its MR.2 form until defence cuts brought about 206 Squadron's final demise in April 2005.

Post-war, Leuchars remained under Coastal Command control until 1950 when, with the jet age beckoning, it was transferred to Fighter Command. The usual array of Cold War RAF jet fighters passed through the airfield, including the Gloster Meteor, de Havilland Vampire, the popular Hawker Hunter and the Gloster Javelin. The iconic English Electric Lightning first arrived in 1964 with 74 Squadron and was in turn replaced by the McDonnell Douglas Phantom. By the

The McDonnell Douglas Phantom served at Leuchars for three decades. The aircraft is an FG.1 of 43 Squadron.

late 1980s the Cold War was coming to an end and the Phantom was withdrawn from RAF service. The Panavia Tornado F.2 took over the UK Air Defence role and today the Tornado F.3 continues to carry out this role with 43(F) and 111(F) Squadrons.

This remarkable airfield's history is so rich that this chapter has only skimmed the surface of what took place during the Second World War. The story of RAF Leuchars could easily fill this book on its own and more!

7
STRAVITHIE

During the early years of the Second World War, large Maintenance Units (MUs) within the RAF needed additional dispersed storage areas for the huge numbers of aircraft that they were handling. A good example of this was 44 MU at Edzell, which needed no fewer than three Satellite Landing Grounds (SLGs) during the war years plus the use of Perth airfield for temporary storage. One of the three SLGs was located at Stravithie, three miles south-east of St Andrews.

Officially opened on 1st May 1941, as 26 SLG, under the command of Plt Off (later Flg Off) R. Cumming, Stravithie was a busy place from the very start. After an inspection by the Officer Commanding 44 MU, Wg Cdr R. W. Thomas OBE, the first airmen were posted to the airfield on 3rd May and all were billeted in St Andrews. A further twenty personnel arrived on 7th May. Guard duties at Stravithie were carried out by The Black Watch. The Army Guard was later accommodated at Bonnytown, a hamlet close to the landing ground.

The first aircraft began to arrive on 9th May 1941. By the end of the first month of operations, 44 aircraft (mainly Hawker Hurricanes and Vickers Wellingtons) were dispersed around the site. Throughout the summer months, Stravithie stood up well to the aircraft movements, which continued at approximately 40 aircraft coming and going per month. By August, the numbers began to fall and with the onset of winter, a decision was made to reduce 26 SLG to Care and Maintenance during this period.

During February 1942 it was also decided to upgrade and improve the facilities at Stravithie. The Ministry of Aircraft Production (MAP) sanctioned the construction of a single 'T'-shaped hard standing, a Tool shed and a Mess Cabin. By the beginning of April the work had been completed, by which time camouflage hedging was also in place

Vickers Wellingtons were one of the first aircraft to be stored by 44 MU from May 1941 at Stravithie.

to disrupt the pattern of the airfield from the air. This must have been very effective because a Miles Magister in difficulties force-landed alongside the runway without realising it was there! After attempting to take off, the Magister struck a tree and crashed. Personnel at the SLG helped the pilot, who luckily was uninjured in the accident. The same month, a Spitfire is recorded as having crashed 600 yds west of the landing ground, but the fate of the pilot and the aircraft is unknown.

The winter of 1941/42 was a hard one, and much of the airfield was covered by snow during this time. Despite this, after an inspection it was found that the runway had stood up very well and preparations began to reopen the SLG.

The improvements at the SLG had not gone unnoticed and, possibly as a result, Sqn Ldr Carter from Montrose visited on 11th May 1942. Montrose was the home of 2 Flying Training School (FTS), which was on the hunt for more landing facilities. However, despite the improvements made to the SLG, Stravithie was not what 2 FTS was looking for.

Following a visit by senior officers from 44 MU, the airfield was reopened on 24th May 1942. The following day, 50 men from the 30th Battalion Highland Regiment began anti-sabotage patrols around the SLG in response to several incidents of forced entry during the previous month in which tools and equipment had been stolen. While the thefts were more likely to have been the work of local opportunists, the possibility of sabotage could never be ruled out and the prevention of it was taken very seriously.

On 29th May 1942 a Boulton Paul Defiant became the only 44 MU aircraft to be involved in an accident at the SLG. The pilot overshot the runway and crashed in a nearby field, fortunately without injury.

During June 1942, 34 aircraft were delivered to the SLG and nineteen were despatched; despite the airfield having being improved, the latter figure proved to be the highest monthly total for the year. A survey of the airfield was also carried out during the month to see if it was fit for night-flying operations. The surveying group was led by Air Vice Marshal Willocks, AOC Flying Training Command, and it is possible that the survey was in actual fact a more serious assessment of how well or otherwise Stravithie could support the activities of 2 FTS at Montrose. Once again, the results could not have been positive because no night-flying training was ever conducted at Stravithie.

The aircraft holding at 26 SLG steadily declined through the summer of 1942; but as with the majority of SLGs elsewhere in Great Britain, plans were by now in place to use 26 SLG for the storage of four-engined aircraft, and feasibility tests began in July. Flt Lt Duffy undertook the first such test on 29th July 1942, when he successfully landed a Handley Page Halifax at Stravithie. The following day saw the arrival of a Short Stirling, flown by Sqn Ldr Sinclair and Plt Off Cheetham, which also landed without trouble. However, despite the fact that Stravithie proved more than capable of handling these large aircraft, none were ever stored on site.

As in the previous year, 26 SLG was closed down for the winter on 30th September 1942. However, there is no evidence that Stravithie was subsequently reopened and no record of any more aircraft being stored there. It is known that the SLG remained under the control of 44 MU until at least the end of the Second World War. Given that Dunino was located only two miles to the east, it is quite possible that increased activity there brought about the early closure of Stravithie. The Westland Lysanders of 309 Squadron based at Dunino did use the 26 SLG site, but apart from this very little further activity seems to have taken place at Stravithie.

By the war's end in Europe, Stravithie was closed down and no further flying would take place at the SLG. Today, the whole site is farmed and can be easily seen in its entirety from the B9131 road. Only a handful of brick buildings were ever constructed but one of these, the

Very few permanent buildings were ever constructed at Stravithie, making the existence of the original Watch Office quite a find. This unique building is deteriorating rapidly and we can only hope that a preservation order can be placed upon it before it disappears. (Author)

Watch Office, stands defiantly very close to the roadside. Converted into a small bungalow during the post-war years, the building is now empty and semi-derelict, so its future looks in doubt.

8
WOODHAVEN

The sight of flying boats landing and taking off from the River Tay dates back to 1918. Literally across the water from Woodhaven, Royal Naval Air Station Dundee was a very busy but short-lived home to several operational squadrons during the final days of the First World War. The River Tay was also the venue for the start of an attempt on a world distance record on 6th October 1938. This involved the Short Mayo composite, which consisted of a modified Short S.23 flying boat (*Maia*) carrying a Short S.20 (*Mercury*) four-engine seaplane; the latter was launched from atop the S.23 in mid-air. The intention was to fly

The Short Mayo composite consisting of a Short S.23 flying boat with the Short S.20 Mercury on its back.

When Norway surrendered in June 1940, four Norwegian Navy Heinkel He 115A-2s escaped to the United Kingdom. One aircraft, later registered as BV186, was flown from Woodhaven. Photographs of Norwegian Navy examples are rare. The example shown is being operated by the Luftwaffe.

non-stop to Cape Town in South Africa but fuel problems resulted in the S.20 landing 500 miles short. Despite this an impressive record was achieved of 6,045 miles flown.

A few miles along the coast, Tayport was also a temporary seaplane base for Short Singapore IIIs and Short Sunderland Is of 210 Squadron, the unit being detached from Pembroke Dock in Pembrokeshire from 29th September to 8th October 1938. Another detachment of 210 Squadron came back to Woodhaven when the Second World War began but by 16th September 1939, they too had returned to Pembroke Dock. There is no reason to doubt that several Sunderland-equipped squadrons passed through Woodhaven during the war years; and 210 Squadron returned again briefly during early 1943, having replaced their Sunderlands with Consolidated Catalinas.

Woodhaven's official beginnings are a little vague but the first aircraft to operate from the new seaplane base on a regular basis was quite unusual. When Norway surrendered on 10th June 1940, six Norwegian Navy Heinkel He 115A-2s attempted to escape German occupation. One escaped to Finland, one was lost without trace over the North Sea and the remaining four managed to make it to Great

Britain. The aircraft were flown to Helensburgh, to where the Marine Aircraft Experimental Establishment (MAEE) had been evacuated from Felixstowe in Suffolk at the outbreak of the Second World War.

Initially, the four He 115A-2s were formed into the Helensburgh Group under the command of Cdr Brugge and still under Norwegian Navy control. The intention was for the aircraft to perform leaflet-dropping sorties over Norwegian cities. However, after evaluation, the four floatplanes were impressed into RAF service and given the serials BV184–187. It was decided instead that the aircraft should be used for covert operations, still with Norwegian crews, both in Norway and the Mediterranean theatre of operations. One of the four aircraft, BV186, was based at Woodhaven and flown by Lt Knut Kavhaugen, who served as a pilot until his death in a Mosquito crash off the Norwegian coast in March 1945. How long BV186 flew from Woodhaven is not known, but the covert operations were soon abandoned and the floatplane was later broken up on the banks of the Tay – the only one of the four He 115A-2s not to have been destroyed in action or by accident.

During February 1942, a brief detachment of 210 Squadron passed through Woodhaven. A single Consolidated Catalina I was subsequently left behind by the unit to form a Norwegian Detachment. The American-built Catalina was a superb aircraft which first flew under the designation PBY-1 in 1935. A multitude of variants followed for the US Navy and in 1939 the Air Ministry's attention was drawn to the twin-engined flying boat. A single example was flown across the Atlantic for evaluation at the MAEE, which at that time was still based at Felixstowe. After testing, an order for 30 Catalina Is was placed; this was increased to 90 upon the outbreak of war.

The Catalina I entered RAF service with 240 Squadron at Stranraer in March 1941 and a total of approximately 640 examples of various Marks were acquired by the RAF for service around the world with eighteen operational squadrons and a host of support and training units. The 'Cat' could carry a bomb load of 4,000 lb or four 325 lb depth charges, had a range of up to 2,760 miles and an amazing endurance of up to 17.6 hours. Superbly reliable, with engine failures almost unheard of, it could land on seas with waves up to six feet high, whereas sea landings by the Sunderland were limited to waves of four feet.

The first Catalina I to be allocated to the Norwegian Flight (W8424/'R') carried the name *Vingtor* beneath the cockpit with a Norwegian national flag painted alongside. The aircraft was quickly

A single Consolidated Catalina I was allocated to the 'Norwegian Flight' at Woodhaven during 1942.

put to work, flying along the Norwegian coast, delivering and picking up agents and supporting the resistance movement. The aircraft also engaged in submarine hunting, convoy escort duties and transport flights to Murmansk in the northern Soviet Union. The small Norwegian Flight's important role was recognised on 7th May 1942 when His Majesty King Haakon VII of Norway visited Woodhaven to inspect the unit.

Other Norwegian units passed through Woodhaven on a regular basis from mid-1942 onwards, including 330 (Norwegian) Squadron, which had just converted to the Catalina III and whose flying boats were regular visitors. On several occasions, the unit's Catalinas began their reconnaissance sorties of the Norwegian coast from Woodhaven. The squadron later converted to the Short Sunderland and it was one of these that caused a commotion on the River Tay in late 1944. The aircraft in question was a Sunderland III (ML819) that broke its moorings on the Tay during a gale on 14th November. It was taken in tow by a Walton-type boat but its towing bar fractured and the giant flying boat drifted into the Tay Bridge. It was then taken under tow by a pinnace which towed the stricken Sunderland to Tayport where the resident Marine Section looked after it throughout the night until the gale subsided the following morning. The Sunderland had in fact suffered only minor damage and was soon back in service with 330 Squadron.

In September 1942, a second Catalina I (*Jøssing*) arrived for service with the Norwegian Flight, followed by a Catalina IB (FP314/'A' *Viking*) in March 1943. Up until then, the Flight was not officially recognised in any capacity, but on 17th February 1943 it became known as 1477 (Norwegian) Flight. Under the command of Cdr F. Lambrechts, the Flight continued its clandestine operations from Woodhaven to Norway. The unit expanded from 16th April when it contributed several personnel to maintain six ex-23 Squadron de Havilland Mosquito IIs at Leuchars. At first the Mosquitos, which were eventually all crewed by Norwegians, carried out Shipping Reconnaissance duties, but as the war progressed they were assigned the more aggressive role of attacking shipping and land targets.

During an Anti-Submarine sweep on 13th April 1943, Sub Lt Anonsen and his crew in *Vingtor* became the first personnel of 1477 (Norwegian) Flight to have a close encounter with the enemy. Just over 200 miles north-north-east of the Shetland Islands at 1539 hours, a U-boat was spotted on the surface, steering westward at approximately seven knots. Within a minute, Anonsen was positioning his Catalina for a depth charge attack on the submarine which remained on the surface, completely oblivious to the presence of the flying boat. As the Catalina swooped closer, the first depth charge exploded 150 ft behind the submarine; then a second exploded directly astern, within 15 ft. A third depth charge fell 60 ft off the starboard quarter and the fourth and final depth charge failed to release. Both of the Catalina's rear blister gunners opened up with their 0.303 machine guns and reported hitting the U-boat several times. By now the submarine was crash-diving in an attempt to escape. After the attack, Sub Lt Anonsen circled back over the area and spotted large bubbles on average 6 ft in diameter and leaving a trail 10 yds wide and 100 yds long. Frustratingly, the Catalina's crew could not confirm, despite the accuracy of their attack, that the U-boat had actually been sunk. A U-boat was lost that day in the Bay of Biscay but none were reported missing in the area that Anonsen had attacked.

The Anonsen crew would get another chance three days later, this time in *Viking*. Once again, on another Anti-Submarine sweep, this time 130 miles north-north-east of the most northerly point of the Shetland Islands, a U-boat periscope was spotted and, without hesitation, Anonsen positioned his Catalina for an attack. All four depth charges were dropped within a space of 100 ft ahead of the periscope and with a depth setting of 25 ft. Due to the position of the aircraft, the explosions could not be seen and after fifteen minutes of circling the area with no sign of any wreckage, the Catalina turned for base. Once again, as with the previous attack, the U-boat had had a very lucky escape.

The title of 1477 (Norwegian) Flight was to be short-lived because on 10th May 1943 the unit was redesignated 333 (Norwegian) Squadron; the fourth Norwegian unit to be formed within the framework of the RAF. The squadron's aircraft continued to be based at two separate locations, the Catalinas at Woodhaven operating as 'A' Flight and the Mosquitos at Leuchars as 'B' Flight.

No more U-boat attacks were recorded until 17th May 1944 when Catalina 'D' (*Jøssing*) caught an enemy vessel on the surface. The U-boat put up a strong defence with its deck gun and the Catalina was seriously damaged and one crew member killed in the process. On return to base, the damage sustained by the Catalina was deemed serious enough to warrant the aircraft being classified as beyond economical repair. Its place was subsequently taken by a Catalina IB (FP183 *Ulabrand*) which, within a few days of arriving at Woodhaven, was in action off the coast of Norway.

Lt C. F. Krafft and crew in *Ulabrand* were on patrol approximately 100 miles west-north-west of Stadlandet on 17th June when they spotted a U-boat (U-423) beneath the surface. The submarine was quickly straddled by four depth charges whose explosions lifted the vessel out of the water. U-423, under the command of Oblt zur See K. Hackländer, stood no chance and thirteen men on board were killed

As new aircraft replaced old and the Flight became 333 Squadron, new marks of the Catalina arrived at Woodhaven, like this MK.IVA.

instantly. A further 40 survivors were seen in the water, but before a rescue could be carried out the icy northern waters had claimed all of their lives.

As aircraft serving with 333 Squadron were replaced or struck off charge, their direct replacements always inherited the previous aircraft's name, complete with a set of Roman numerals. For example, *Vingtor* was replaced five times, so that when the war came to an end the squadron was operating a Catalina IVB (JX573/'B') named *Vingtor V*. (This policy applied to all four Catalinas, the names of which live on today with the current 333 Skvadron, Royal Norwegian Air Force, which now operates another American anti-submarine aircraft type, the Lockheed P-3C and P-3N Orion.)

With the Germans on the back foot in Norway, much of 333 Squadron's time was taken up flying transport missions. When hostilities in Europe ceased, 333 Squadron moved its four Catalinas to Fornebu near Oslo on 11th June 1945, just four days after King Haakon VII had returned to Norway from exile in Great Britain. The squadron was officially disbanded on 21st November 1945 and transferred to the Royal Norwegian Air Force. The squadron's trusty Catalinas, all of which still belonged to the RAF, were handed back; but the squadron continued to function, making good use of a variety of captured German Arado Ar 196A-3 floatplanes and Dornier Do 24T-3 flying boats.

The exact date of Woodhaven's closure is unknown but with 333 Squadron's departure, no other units were recorded as having used the flying boat station. It can only be presumed that, by the end of June 1945, Woodhaven was closed and consigned to history. Today, there is no trace of the site which would have had only a few buildings on the shore and possibly a slipway. The latter, if one actually existed at all, cannot be found today. Nevertheless, looking across the River Tay, it is not too difficult to imagine Sunderlands and Catalinas on the step and about to take to the air.

9
CIVILIANS AT WAR

Serious preparations for a second world conflict began in early 1939, although tension across Europe had been high for many years previous. Throughout Fife and Central, systems were being put into place and tested, especially with regard to Air Raid Precautions (ARP). It was obvious that the enemy would attack from the air first followed by the inevitable attempt at an invasion. The latter would be met by a formidable array of coastal defences, ranging from pillboxes to highly complex coastal batteries. Beaches were quickly covered with obstacles ranging from barbed wire to huge concrete blocks, all intended to stop or at least disrupt the progress of an enemy tank. Mines were also planted along the coastline, which meant that virtually all the Fife coast was now strictly out of bounds.

It was ARP that would be the first event to affect the civilian population. Anderson shelters began to appear in people's gardens, while communal shelters were constructed in the larger towns and cities to protect large numbers of civilians. Gas masks were issued to every man, woman and child because senior military advisers were convinced that Germany would use gas as a weapon, as it had done during the First World War. Although during the earlier conflict the use of gas was contained within the trenches, it was thought that Germany's huge and much-expanded air force would drop gas canisters over Great Britain. Thankfully this never happened and as the war progressed, more and more civilians relegated their gas masks to the back of the cupboard.

During August 1939, many ARP exercises were carried out across Scotland to test how quickly posts could be manned, the sounding of air raid sirens and the reaction times of the civilian population. With the war only weeks away these exercises proved to be very timely.

The evacuation of school children from Edinburgh began on 2nd September 1939. The first batch of 300 children arrived in Dunfermline from where they were sent to various homes throughout West Fife. This continued for many weeks, but often in reverse when many civilians decided, perhaps prematurely, that it was safe enough to return to the cities. Being so rural, Fife received many thousands of evacuees, often referred to as 'wee vaccies', from all the major cities in Scotland. Many more arrived from the northeast of England, especially Newcastle upon Tyne which, like Glasgow and Clydebank, was bombed heavily during the early years of the war.

Fife as a whole did not suffer a great deal of bombing but obviously the Rosyth Naval Dockyard, located on the northern bank of the Firth of Forth, was bombed on many occasions. Warships anchored in the Forth were generally the priority targets for the Luftwaffe which suffered heavy losses in their efforts to sink these ships. To raise morale, His Majesty King George VI visited Rosyth Naval Dockyard on 6th March 1941 to decorate several Norwegian and British sailors who had served with distinction during the Norwegian campaign. While military casualties were suffered, civilian deaths and injuries were mercifully low in number, with only a handful recorded in Fife during the whole of the Second World War. Deaths from walking into minefields along the coast and fatalities on the roads due to the blackout were considerably more than those inflicted by enemy action.

The arrival of rationing in people's daily lives brought about a resurgence in vegetable gardens and allotments throughout the country. Rationing was introduced from January 1940, and with it came the daily chore of dealing with ration cards, joining queues and chasing items that, only a few months earlier, were easy to purchase. Butter, sugar, bacon and ham were the first items to be rationed; but potatoes, bread, fish and offal were in plentiful supply, so these items became a staple part of the diet. 'Dig for Victory' was the government's campaign to encourage people to turn their gardens into vegetable patches and the addition of fresh vegetables to dinner plates made life more bearable.

Several 'War Weapons Weeks' were organised throughout the Second World War to raise funds for military equipment. The people of Dunfermline alone raised over half a million pounds during one particular fund-raising week in 1941. The chairman of the Scottish War Savings Committee, Lord Alness congratulated the town for a magnificent achievement. Other fund-raising events such as 'Warship Week', 'Tanks for Attack' and 'Salute the Soldier' raised large amounts of money in support of the war effort.

In April 1942, the Women's Timber Corps (WTC) was formed in England, followed the next month by Scotland's own WTC which was part of the Women's Land Army. The WTC in Scotland had its own identity and uniform and recruited girls and women from the age of seventeen upwards, although some as young as fourteen managed to join.

Affectionately known as the 'Lumberjills', they were trained at various camps including Shadford Lodge near Brechin, and many were posted to Fife. The Lumberjills replaced the many men who had been called up into military service. Their work included felling, snedding (the removal of branches from a felled tree), loading lorries and trains and operating sawmills all over Scotland. In August 1946, the WTC was disbanded and every woman had to hand back her uniform. In 2006 a study was carried out to erect a memorial to the work of the Lumberjills in Scotland; and the Forestry Commission of Scotland commissioned Fife-based artist Malcolm Robertson to produce a fitting memorial to the Lumberjills. On 10th October 2007 a beautiful statue, a life-sized bronze sculpture of a member of the WTC, was unveiled at David Marshall Lodge near Aberfoyle in Stirlingshire in memory of the 5,000 women who served with the corps.

Fife had a high concentration of coal mines within its borders and very early in the war the government underestimated the importance of coal for the war effort. By 1943, over 36,000 coal miners across Great Britain had been conscripted into the armed forces, many of whom were highly experienced workers. Initially the government made a plea for those liable for conscription to work in the mines, but very few responded while much cleaner work was in plentiful supply. By December 1943, the situation was becoming desperate and it was decided that a percentage of all conscripts would be diverted to work in the mines. Once again it was up to Ernest Bevin to announce: 'We need 720,000 men continuously employed in this industry. This is where you boys come in. Our fighting men will not be able to achieve their purpose unless we get an adequate supply of coal.' From this speech, the title of 'Bevin Boys' was given to all those who served down the coal mines rather than in the armed services.

Thirteen Government Training Centre Collieries were established throughout Great Britain to train the Bevin Boys. The only one in Scotland was located at Muircockhall near Dunfermline with accommodation established at the Miners Hostel at Townhill; the latter was very similar to a military-style camp. The miners were charged 25 shillings per week for the accommodation out of an average weekly salary of three pounds and ten shillings. Training lasted for four weeks, broken down into 25% classroom lectures, 20% surface work, 30% underground and 25% physical training. When the training was complete, the miner was transferred to a colliery, usually in the same region as the training pit – which in Muircockhall's case would mean anywhere in Scotland.

Approximately 10% of all eligible conscripts between the ages of 18 and 25 were diverted to work in the coal mines. The scheme lasted from early 1944 through to 1948, by which time nearly 48,000 Bevin Boys had been trained. They were not officially recognised for their efforts until the Queen's Speech during the 50th Anniversary of VE Day in 1995; and it was not until March 2008 that a badge was issued for all surviving Bevin Boys in recognition of their service.

Many companies changed their production to war work, employing a large number of civilian workers in the process. Several military establishments employed civilians, including Rosyth Naval Dockyard and, more relevant to this book, the Royal Naval Aircraft Repair Yard at Donibristle. The origins of the repair yard lay in the post-First World War period, but it underwent significant expansion during the Second World War. Many skilled workers were actually transferred from Rosyth to retrain in aircraft trades and by 1940 the repair yard employed at least 450 civilians.

The repair yard was expanded again in 1941 and by the end of that year 320 aircraft had passed through for either repair or modification work. The upward trend continued until 1945, by which time 7,000 aircraft had passed through. At its peak in late 1944, the repair yard employed over 3,000 people, 2,000 of whom were civilians.

By late 1944, with the Allied forces steadily pushing closer to Berlin, life on the Home Front began to improve. ARP restrictions began to lessen as the threat of enemy bombers over the area diminished. Blackout restrictions were also downgraded to a 'dim-out' in response to the lack of enemy activity. Mine-clearance operations by both Army and RAF Regiment units cleared many of Fife's beaches of the deadly weapons many months before the war's end. The Home Guard was also disbanded on 1st November 1944, such was the optimism that the end of the war was close. Frustratingly it continued until 8th May 1945, much longer than had been anticipated, resulting in a large number of unnecessary deaths and injuries on both sides.

VE (Victory in Europe) Day was celebrated by all throughout Great Britain with great enthusiasm, which brought the population together to a degree that has not and probably never will be repeated. Both Winston Churchill and His Majesty King George VI praised the civilian population for their resilience and hard work against the Nazi machine. Over 65,000 British civilians had lost their lives during the Second World War with a further 86,000 wounded.

APPENDIX

Units and their aircraft located at airfields in Fife and the
Central Region during the Second World War

CRAIL

800 Sqn From HMS *Ark Royal* 8th Oct 40 with Roc. To Prestwick 27th Oct 40.

827 Sqn From Yeovilton 2nd Nov 40 with Albacore I. To HMS *Argus* (DLT) 9th Mar 41. To Stornoway (18 Gp) 14th Mar 41.

829 Sqn From St Eval 3rd Nov 40 with Albacore I. To HMS *Formidable* 15th Nov 40.

785 Sqn Formed Crail (satellite Dunino) 4th Nov 40 with Shark II, Swordfish I/II, Albacore I, Tiger Moth II, Barracuda I/II/TR.III, Master I, Avenger I/II, Anson I. Disbanded 1st Mar 46.

786 Sqn Formed Crail (satellite Dunino) 21st Nov 40 with Albacore I, Swordfish I/II, Chesapeake I, Tiger Moth II, Barracuda I/II, Anson I. Disbanded 21st Dec 45.

812 Sqn Det 3 From North Coates (?) 16th Jan 41 with Swordfish I. To North Coates (?) 2nd Mar 41.

828 Sqn Det from Campbeltown 23rd Jan 41 with Albacore I. To Campbeltown 23rd Mar 41.

43 Sqn Det from Drem 22nd Feb 41 with Hurricane I. To Drem 1st Mar 41.

817 Sqn Formed Crail 15th Mar 41 with Albacore I. To HMS *Furious* 15th Jul 41.

831 Sqn Formed Crail 1st Apr 41 with Albacore I. To Machrihanish 26th Aug 41.

770 Sqn From Donibristle 1st Jun 41 with Roc I, Skua II, Proctor II, Blenheim I, Botha I, Chesapeake I, Defiant TT.I, Seafire L.IIC, Martinet TT.I. To Dunino 29th Jan 44.

828 Sqn From HMS *Victorious* 8th Aug 41 with Albacore I. To HMS *Argus* 26th Sep 41.

820 Sqn From Lee-on-Solent 26th Sep 41 with Albacore I. To Hatston 1st Nov 41.

823 Sqn Reformed Crail 1st Nov 41 with Swordfish I. To Fraserburgh 6th Dec 41.

819 Sqn From Lee-on-Solent 8th Dec 41 with Swordfish I. To Twatt 27th Jan 42.

833 Sqn From Lee-on-Solent 5th Feb 42 with Swordfish I. To Hatston 21st Mar 42.

822 Sqn From Hatston 20th Mar 42 with Swordfish II, Albacore I. To Donibristle 2nd May 42.

144, 415 and **455 Sqns** Various detachments from Leuchars Apr to Sep 42 with Hampden TB.Is.

309 Sqn 'B' Flt From Dunino 15th Jun 42 with Mustang I. To Gatwick Nov 42.

832 Sqn From HMS *Victorious* 21st Aug 42 with Albacore I. To Machrihanish 10th Sep 42.

831 Sqn From HMS *Indomitable* 27th Aug 42 with Albacore I. To Lee-on-Solent 27th Dec 42.

832 Sqn From Machrihanish 20th Sep 42 with Albacore I. Det 3 to Manston 23rd Sep to 22nd Nov 42. To Machrihanish 24th Sep 42.

836 Sqn From HMS *Indomitable* 24th Sep 42 with Swordfish I. To Lee-on-Solent 28th Oct 42.

832 Sqn From HMS *Victorious* 22nd Nov 42 with Albacore I. To Machrihanish 8th Dec 42.

834 Sqn From HMS *Archer* 2nd Dec 42 with Swordfish I/II. To Exeter 9th Feb 43.

837 Sqn From Hatston 30th Dec 42 with Swordfish I. 'A' Flt to HMS *Argus* 15th Jan 43; returned to Crail via North Front and HMS *Argus* 9th Feb 43. 'B' Flt to HMS *Dasher* 22nd Jan 43. To Dunino 25th Feb 43.

Fleet Air Arm Mobile Workshop Unit Formed Crail 1943 in support of HMS *Jackdaw* and *Dunino*. Disbanded 1944 (?).

778 Sqn From Arbroath 5th Mar 43 with Swordfish I/II, Walrus I, Fulmar I/II, Spitfire IX, Martlet IV, Barracuda I/II, Seafire IB/IIC/III, Avenger I, Sea Hurricane IB/IIC/III, Sea Otter I, Helldiver I, Hellcat I. 'B' Flt det in HMS *Pretoria* 14th Aug 43 to 23rd May 45. To Arbroath 15th Aug 44.

810 Sqn From HMS *Illustrious* 18th Oct 43 with Barracuda II. To Machrihanish 4th Nov 43.

811 Sqn Fighter Flt From HMS *Vindex* 25th Nov 43 with Wildcat IV. To Stretton 10th Dec 43.

758 Sqn 'E' Flt From Hinstock 20th Jan 44 with Oxford. To Hinstock 26th Apr 44.

822 Sqn From Fearn 1st Feb 44 with Barracuda II. To Burscough 18th Feb 44.

826 Sqn From Lee-on-Solent 3rd Feb 44 with Barracuda II. To HMS *Indefatigable* 10th Jun 44.

820 Sqn From Lee-on-Solent (transit) 24th Feb 44 with Barracuda II. To HMS *Indefatigable* 10th Jun 44.

Air Torpedo Development Unit From ? Apr 44. Evacuated during invasion period. To ? Aug 44.

816 Sqn From Machrihanish 17th Apr 44 with Swordfish II, Wildcat V. To Perranporth 20th Apr 44.

812 Sqn From Stretton 28th Jun 44 with Barracuda II. To Burscough 7th Sep 44.

711 Sqn Reformed Crail 9th Sep 44 with Barracuda II, Reliant I, Anson I/ASV, Avenger I/II. Disbanded 21st Dec 45.

DONIBRISTLE

767 Sqn Formed Donibristle 24th May 39 (ex-811 Sqn) with Swordfish I, Shark II, Albacore I, Moth. Dets (DLT) in HMS *Furious* 28th Jun to 7th Jul and 26th Sep to 9th Oct 39. To HMS *Argus* 8th Jul 40.

769 Sqn Formed Donibristle 24th May 39 (ex-801 Sqn) with Skua II, Roc I, Sea Gladiator. Dets (DLT) in HMS *Furious* 15th to 22nd Jun, 17th to 26th Jul, 19th to 23rd Sep 39. Disbanded 1st Dec 39.

801 Sqn Reformed Donibristle 15th Jan 40 with Skua II. To Evanton 2nd Feb 40.

Donibristle Comm Flt Formed by Apr 40 with Proctor, DH.86, Rapide. Disbanded Dec 40.

2 AACU 'D' Flt From Gosport 17th Apr 40 with Gladiator I/II. To Gosport Mar 41.

816 Sqn From Campbeltown 3rd May 40 with Swordfish I. To Campbeltown 17th May 40.

805 Sqn Formed Donibristle 4th May 40 with Roc I. To Lee-on-Solent 7th May 40.

701 Sqn Reformed Donibristle 7th May 40 with Walrus. To HMS *Glorious* 9th May 40.

771 Sqn 'X' Flt Formed Donibristle 26th May 40 with Roc I. Redesignated 770 Sqn 1st Jan 41.

701 Sqn From Hatston 16th Jun 40 with Walrus. To HMS *Argus* 23rd Jun 40.

806 Sqn From HMS *Illustrious* 24th Jul 40 with Skua II, Roc I, Fulmar I. To HMS *Illustrious* 21st Aug 40.

806 Sqn Det 10 From HMS *Illustrious* 19th Aug 40 with Fulmar I. To HMS *Illustrious* 21st Aug 40.

271 Sqn Det from Doncaster Oct 40 to Dec 41 with Albatross, Bombay, Harrow.

808 Sqn From Castletown 2nd Oct 40 with Fulmar I. To HMS *Ark Royal* 31st Oct 40.

803 Sqn From HMS *Ark Royal* 8th Oct 40 with Skua II, Fulmar I. To HMS *Formidable* 27th Nov 40.

820 Sqn From HMS *Ark Royal* 8th Oct 40 with Swordfish I. To Campbeltown 23rd Oct 40.

701 Sqn From HMS *Argus* 26th Oct 40 with Walrus. To Stornoway 6th Nov 40.

825 Sqn From HMS *Furious* (transit) 6th Nov 40 with Swordfish I. To Lee-on-Solent 7th Nov 40.

781/782 Sqn Reformed at Donibristle 1st Dec 40 from a Comms Flight. Also known as the Northern Communication Squadron. Detachments to Inverness 22nd Jan 42 to 24th Aug and 27th July 44 to 27th July 45.

821 Sqn 'X' Flt From Hatston 2nd Dec 40 with Swordfish I. To Prestwick 15th Dec 40.

802 Sqn From Hatston 9th Dec 40 with Martlet I. To Machrihanish 22nd Jun 41.

770 Sqn Reformed Donibristle (from 'X' Flt 771 Sqn) as an FRU 1st Jan 41 with Roc I. To Crail 1st Jun 41.

801 Sqn Det 6 From St Merryn 18th Jan 41 with Skua II, Sea Hurricane I. To St Eval 26th Jan 41.

801 Sqn From Hatston 14th Feb 41 with Skua II, Sea Hurricane I. To West Freugh 18th Feb 41.

825 Sqn Det 6 Det from Arbroath 6th Mar 41 with Swordfish I. To Campbeltown 11th Apr 41.

828 Sqn From Campbeltown 17th Mar 41 with Albacore I. To Hatston 21st Mar 41.

701 Sqn From Hooton Park 22nd Mar 41 with Walrus. Disbanded 8th Jun 41.

800 Sqn 'X' Flt From Lee-on-Solent 2nd May 41 with Fulmar I. To HMS *Victorious* 11th May 41.

827 Sqn From Machrihanish 5th Jun 41 with Albacore I. To Machrihanish 27th Jun 41.

821 Sqn From Detling (transit) 14th Jul 41 with Swordfish I. To Hatston 15th Jul 41.

882 Sqn Formed Donibristle 15th Jul 41 with Martlet I, Sea Hurricane IB. To St Merryn 3rd Nov 41.

817 Sqn From HMS *Victorious* 13th Oct 41 with Albacore I. Det 4 in HMS *Victorious* 19th to 26th Oct 41. To Hatston 26th Oct 41.

802 Sqn From HMS *Audacity* 17th Oct 41 with Martlet I/II. To HMS *Audacity* 28th Oct 41.

884 Sqn Reformed Donibristle 1st Nov 41 with Fulmar II. To St Merryn 1st Jan 42.

808 Sqn Reformed Donibristle 1st Jan 42 with Fulmar II. To St Merryn 17th Mar 42.

886 Sqn Formed Donibristle 15th Mar 42 with Fulmar II. To St Merryn 23rd May 42.

819 Sqn From Hatston 26th Mar 42 with Swordfish I. To Machrihanish 16th Apr 42.

Ferry Pool Donibristle Formed Apr 42 with Fulmar, Dominie, Proctor, Reliant, Tiger Moth, Swordfish, Traveller, Walrus, Seafire.

822 Sqn From Crail 2nd May 42 with Albacore I. To Machrihanish 6th Jun 42.

758 Sqn Reformed Donibristle 25th May 42 with Oxford. To Hinstock 15th Aug 42.

893 Sqn Formed Donibristle 15th Jun 42 with Martlet I, Fulmar I. Det in HMS *Archer* 1st to 13th Jul 42. To St Merryn 23rd Aug 42.

802 Sqn From Peterhead 6th Jul 42 with Sea Hurricane IB. To Machrihanish 13th Jul 42.

882 Sqn Reformed Donibristle 7th Sep 42 with Martlet IV. To Skaebrae 1st Oct 42.

888 Sqn From HMS *Formidable* 21st Sep 42 with Martlet II. To Hatston 8th Oct 42.

891 Sqn From HMS *Dasher* 18th Nov 42 with Sea Hurricane IIC. To Machrihanish 10th Dec 42.

804 Sqn From HMS *Dasher* 19th Nov 42 with Sea Hurricane IIC. To Machrihanish 11th Dec 42.

881 Sqn 'B' Flt From Kirkistown 19th Dec 42 with Martlet II. To Kirkistown 30th Dec 42.

881 Sqn 'B' Flt From Kirkistown 4th Jan 43 with Martlet II. Disbanded into 890 Sqn 8th Jan 43.

890 Sqn From HMS *Battler* 8th Jan 43 with Martlet IV. To Machrihanish 4th Mar 43.

890 Sqn From HMS *Argus* 25th Mar 43 with Martlet IV. To Hatston 28th Mar 43.

800 Sqn From HMS *Unicorn* 16th Apr 43 with Sea Hurricane IIB/C. To Hatston 30th Apr 32.

Donibristle Station Flight Formed May 43 with Swordfish, Tiger Moth, Dominie, Oxford. Disbanded Feb 46.

808 Sqn From HMS *Battler* 7th May 43 with Spitfire VB/hooked, Seafire L.IIC. Det 3 in HMS *Battler* 7th to 11th May 43. To Yeovilton 20th May 43.

800 Sqn From Hatston 8th May 43 with Sea Hurricane IIB/C. To Eglinton 3rd Jun 43.

860 Sqn Formed Donibristle 15th Jun 43 with Swordfish I. To Hatston 19th Jul 43.

825 Sqn From Stornoway (transit) 14th Jul 43 with Swordfish II. To Stretton 15th Jul 43.

824 Sqn From HMS *Unicorn* 31st Jul 43 with Swordfish II. To Machrihanish 18th Aug 43.

813 Sqn Reformed Donibristle 1st Nov 43 with Swordfish II. To Dunino 13th Dec 43.

825 Sqn From Belfast 5th Nov 43 with Swordfish I/II. To Inskip 14th Nov 43.

811 Sqn From HMS *Biter* 25th Nov 43 with Swordfish II. To Inskip 12th Dec 43.

816 Sqn From HMS *Tracker* 28th Dec 43 with Swordfish II. To HMS *Chaser* 19th Jan 44.

890 Sqn From Eglinton 29th Jan 44 with Wildcat V. To HMS *London* 17th Feb 44.

824 Sqn From HMS *Striker* 19th Feb 44 with Swordfish II, Sea Hurricane IIC. To HMS *Striker* 29th Feb 44.

819 Sqn Det 3 From HMS *Activity* 21st Feb 44 with Wildcat. To HMS *Activity* 25th Mar 44.

816 Sqn From HMS *Chaser* 10th Mar 44 with Swordfish II, Wildcat V. To Machrihanish 31st Mar 44.

816 Sqn Fighter Flight From Renfrew 21st Mar 44. To Machrihanish 31st Mar 44.

827 Sqn From HMS *Furious* 7th Apr 44 with Barracuda II. To HMS *Furious* 20th Apr 44.

830 Sqn From HMS *Furious* 7th Apr 44 with Barracuda II. To HMS *Furious* 20th Apr 44.

784 Sqn Det from HMS *Vindex* 28th Apr 44 (disembarked (where?) 23rd Apr 44) with Fulmar IINF, Reliant I, Anson I, Firefly INF. Det disbanded Donibristle 20th Apr 45.

1770 Sqn From HMS *Indefatigable* 25th Jul 44 with Firefly I. To Burscough 27th Jul 44.

1770 Sqn From Ayr 31st Jul 44 with Firefly I. To Kinloss 1st Aug 44.

828 Sqn From HMS *Formidable* 2nd Sep 44 with Barracuda II. To Machrihanish 13th Sep 44.

1841 Sqn From HMS *Formidable* 2nd Sep 44 with Corsair II. To HMS *Formidable* 16th Sep 44.

1842 Sqn From HMS *Formidable* 2nd Sep 44 with Corsair II. To HMS *Formidable* 16th Sep 44.

739 Sqn From Worthy Down 5th Oct 44 with Oxford I, Anson I. Disbanded Donibristle to become 'C' Flt 778 Sqn 7th Mar 45.

700 Sqn Reformed Donibristle 11th Oct 44 with Master II. To Worthy Down 7th Nov 44.

1820 Sqn From Burscough 23rd Oct 44 with Helldiver I. Det in HMS *Speaker* 29th to 30th Oct 44. To Hatston 31st Oct 44.

1820 Sqn From Hatston 1st Dec 44 with Helldiver I. To Burscough 4th Dec 44.

DUNINO

614 Sqn 'B' Flt Det from Macmerry Apr 41 with Lysander.

309 Sqn From Renfrew 8th May 41 with Lysander III, Mustang I. Dets Gatwick, Longman, Campbeltown, Inverness, Findo Gask. 'B' Flt (Mustang I) to Crail Jun to Sep 42. To Findo Gask 26th Nov 42.

737 Sqn Formed Dunino 22nd Feb 43 with Walrus. Disbanded Dunino 28th Sep 43.

825 Sqn From Worthy Down 3rd Feb 43 with Swordfish I/II. To Machrihanish 9th Mar 43.

837 Sqn 'A' Flt From Crail 25th Feb 43 with Swordfish I. Squadron reunited Dunino 29th Mar 43.

837 Sqn 'D' Flt From Hatston 29th Mar 43 with Swordfish. Squadron reunited Dunino 29th Mar 43. To Machrihanish 14th Apr 43.

824 Sqn From Machrihanish 16th Mar 43 with Swordfish II. To Machrihanish 23rd Mar 43.

827 Sqn From Lee-on-Solent 24th Apr 43 with Barracuda I/II. To Machrihanish 12th Aug 43.

778 Sqn Det from Crail Jun 43 with Barracuda.

860 Sqn From Hatston 15th Aug 43 with Swordfish I. To Machrihanish 3rd Nov 43.

833 Sqn From Machrihanish 6th Oct 43 with Swordfish II. To Maydown 15th Dec 43.

813 Sqn From Donibristle 13th Dec 43 with Swordfish II. To Inskip 20th Jan 44.

838 Sqn From HMS *Nairana* 16th Jan 44 with Swordfish II. To Inskip 6th Feb 44.

770 Sqn From Crail 29th Jan 44 with Martinet TT.I, Blenheim IV, Hurricane IIC. To Drem 25th Jul 44.

820 Sqn From Machrihanish (transit) 18th Oct 44 with Barracuda II, Avenger I. To Lee-on-Solent 19th Oct 44.

GRANGEMOUTH

35 E&RFTS Formed Grangemouth 1st May 39 with Tiger Moth, Anson, Hind, Audax. Disbanded 3rd Sep 39.

10 CANS Formed Grangemouth 1st Sep 39 with Anson I. Redesignated 10 AONS 1st Nov 39.

602 Sqn From Abbotsinch 7th Oct 39 with Spitfire I. To Drem 13th Oct 39.

141 Sqn From Turnhouse 19th Oct 39 with Gladiator I, Blenheim IF, Defiant I. To Prestwick 13th to 22nd Feb 40. To Turnhouse 28th Jun 40.

10 AONS Formed Grangemouth from 10 CANS 1st Nov 39 with Anson I. Disbanded into 1 AONS at Prestwick 27th Nov 39.

614 Sqn From Odiham 8th Jun 40 with Lysander II. Dets Evanton, Montrose, Longman, Dumfries, Tangmere. To Macmerry 4th Mar 41.

263 Sqn From Drem 28th Jun 40 with Hurricane I, Whirlwind I. Det Montrose Jul 40. To Drem 2nd Sep 40.

141 Sqn Det from Prestwick Jul to Aug 40 with Defiant I.

58 OTU Formed Grangemouth 21st Oct 40 with Master I/II/III, Spitfire I/II/V, Battle I, Lysander I/III, Dominie, Tiger Moth. Dets Macmerry Dec 4? to Apr 4? and Ayr Oct 4? to Oct 4?. Redesignated 2 CTW 5th Oct 43.

Roc Flt Det from Odiham Nov 40 (attached to 614 Sqn) with Roc.

4 ADF Formed Grangemouth 13th Apr 41 with Dominie. To Turnhouse 7th Jan 42.

2 CTW Formed Grangemouth 5th Oct 43 from 58 OTU with Spitfire I/IIA/V, Master III. Redesignated 2 TEU 15th Oct 43.

2 TEU Formed Grangemouth 15th Oct 43 from 2 CTW with Hurricane I/IV/X, Spitfire I/IIA/V, Martinet TT.I, Master III, Tiger Moth. Det (Spitfire) Hutton Cranswick 29th May to 13th Jun 44. Disbanded 25th Jun 44.

14 MU Aircraft Equipment Depot sub-depot for main unit at Carlisle 12th Oct 44 to 31st Aug 49.

243 MU Air Ammunition Park satellite for main unit at Kirknewton from 1st Nov 44. Disbanded 7th Jan 52.

6 GS Formed Grangemouth Feb 45 with Cadet I/II/TX.3. To Turnhouse Jan 46.

LEUCHARS

Temporary Armament Training Station, Leuchars Formed Leuchars in 25 Gp (range at Tentsmuir) with Henley, Gordon. Disbanded into 8 AOS at Evanton.

224 Sqn From Thornaby 26th Mar 38 with Anson I, Hudson I/III. Dets Abbotsinch, Wick. To Limavady 15th Apr 41.

233 Sqn From Montrose 10th Oct 38 with Anson I, Hudson I, Blenheim IV. Dets Montrose, Bircham Newton. To Aldergrove 3rd Aug 40.

269 Sqn One Flight from Wick 10th Oct 39 with Anson I.

612 Sqn One Flight from Wick 22nd Oct 39 with Anson I.

605 Sqn Attached from Tangmere 11th Feb 40 with Hurricane I. To Wick 28th Feb 40.

18 Gp Comm Flt From Turnhouse 13th May 40 with Proctor, Magister, Walrus, Mentor. To Turnhouse 18th Nov 59.

233 Sqn From Aldergrove with Hudson I. To Aldergrove 8th Dec 40.

320 Sqn From Carew Cheriton with Anson I, Hudson I. Det Silloth. To Carew Cheriton 18th Jan 41.

65 Sqn From Turnhouse 8th Nov 40 with Hurricane I. To Tangmere 29th Nov 40.

72 Sqn From Coltishall 29th Nov 40 with Spitfire I. To Acklington 15th Dec 40.

10 BAT Flt Formed Leuchars 9th Dec 40 with Wellington I/IC. Redesignated 1510 BAT Flt 19th May 42 with Oxford, Anson I. Became 1510 BABS Flt 25th Dec 42. To Squires Gate 15th Aug 44.

St Andrews UAS Formed at Leuchars 23rd Jan 41 with Tiger Moth, Oxford. To Crail Mar 53.

86 Sqn From Gosport 2nd Feb 41 with Blenheim IV. To Wattisham 3rd Mar 41.

42 Sqn From Wick 1st Mar 42 with Beaufort I/II. Dets North Coates, Sumburgh, Coltishall, St Eval, Wick. To Far East (by sea) 18th Jun 42.

107 Sqn From Wattisham with Blenheim IV. To Great Massingham 3rd May 41.

320 Sqn From Carew Cheriton 21st Mar 41 with Anson I, Hudson I. To Bircham Newton 21st Apr 42.

114 Sqn From Thornaby 13th May 41 with Blenheim IV. To West Raynham 19th Jul 41.

1420 Flt From Thornaby via Selkirk Jun 41 with Blenheim IV. To West Raynham 19th Jul 41.

489 Sqn Formed Leuchars 12th Aug 41 with Beaufort I, Blenheim IV. To Thorney Island 8th Mar 42.

18 Gp APC Formed Leuchars Oct 41 with Lysander II. Redesignated 3 APC Dec 41.

3 APC Formed Leuchars 5th Nov 41 with Lysander II, Martinet TT.I. Disbanded 12th Dec 45.

105 Sqn Dets from Horsham St Faith Dec 41 to Sep 42 with Mosquito IV.

217 Sqn From Thorney Island 1st Mar 42 with Beaufort II. Dets Sumburgh, Skitten. En route Far East via Luqa, Malta 7th May 42.

144 Sqn From North Luffenham 17th Apr 42 with Hampden I, Beaufighter VIC. To Tain 8th Apr 43.

455 Sqn From Wigsley 28th Apr 42 with Hampden I, Beaufighter X. Dets Sumburgh Vaenga, Benbecula, Tain, Wick. To Langham 14th Apr 44.

415 Sqn Det from Wick Aug 42 with Hampden I.

489 Sqn Det from Wick Sep to Oct 42 with Hampden I.

415 Sqn From Tain 6th Sep 42 with Hampden. Dets St Eval, Thorney Island. To Thorney Island 11th Nov 42.

544 Sqn Dets from Benson Oct 42 to Mar 43 with Anson I, Maryland I, Wellington IV, Spitfire IV.

489 Sqn From Wick 6th Oct 43 with Hampden I, Beaufighter X. To Langham 8th Apr 44.

540 Sqn Formed Leuchars 19th Oct 42 with Spitfire IV, Mosquito I/IV/VIII/IX. To Benson 29th Feb 44.

23 MTU Formed Leuchars Dec 42. Possibly disbanded Leuchars Dec 43.

2 TRS Formed Leuchars 1st Jan 43. Disbanded 9th Apr 43.

235 Sqn From Chivenor 21st Jan 43 with Beaufighter VI. Dets Sumburgh, Tain, St Eval. To Portreath 29th Aug 43.

1477 (Norwegian) Flt Formed Leuchars 16th Apr 43 to maintain Mosquitos and Beaufighters of 235 Sqn. Disbanded into 333 Sqn 5th May 43.

333 Sqn 'B' Flt Formed Leuchars 5th May 43 with Mosquito II/VI. To Banff 1st Sep 44.

281 Sqn Det from Tiree Mar 44 to Jan 45 with Warwick I.

Air Torpedo Development Unit Apr to 12th Aug 44.

206 Sqn From St Eval 11th Jul 44 with Liberator VI/VIII. To Oakington 31st Jul 45.

547 Sqn From St Eval 28th Sep 44 with Liberator VI/VIII. Disbanded 4th Jun 45.

STRAVITHIE

26 SLG Opened 1st May 44 for 44 MU (Edzell). Closed by Sep 42.

309 Sqn Dets from Dunino summer 41 with Lysander IIIA.

WOODHAVEN

210 Sqn From Pembroke Dock early Sep 43 with Sunderland I. To Pembroke Dock by 16th Sep 39.

210 Sqn Det from Pembroke Dock early Feb 42 with Catalina IIA/IIIA. To Pembroke Dock late 43.

1477 Flt Formed Woodhaven 8th Feb 43 with Catalina. Redesignated 333 Sqn 10th May 43.

333 Sqn Formed Woodhaven ('A' Flt) and Leuchars ('B' Flt) 10th May 43 with Catalina IB/IV ('A' Flt) and Mosquito ('B' Flt). 'A' Flt det to Sullom Voe. To Fornebu, Norway Jan 45.

BIBLIOGRAPHY

Francis, P., *British Military Airfield Architecture*, PSL
Halley, J. J. *The K File*, Air Britain
Halley, J. J., *The Squadrons of the Royal Air Force*, Air Britain
Jefford, C. G., *RAF Squadrons*, Airlife
Fife, M., *Crail and Dunino*, GSM
Fife, M., *Donibristle, Airfield Focus No. 52*, GSM
McNeill, R., *RAF Coastal Command Losses 39–41*, Midland
Mitchell, A., *New Zealander in the Air War*, George G. Harrap
Rawlings, J. D. R., *Fighter Squadrons of the RAF*, Macdonald
Smith, D. J., *Action Stations No. 7*, PSL
Sturtivant, R., *FAA Fixed-Wing Aircraft since 1946*, Air Britain
Sturtivant, R., *RAF Flying Training and Support Units*, Air Britain
Thetford, O., *Aircraft of the RAF since 1918*, PSL
Tunnicliffe, D. DFC, *From Bunnies to Beaufighters*
Willis, S., & Hollis, B., *Military Airfields in the British Isles*, Enthusiasts
    Publications

TNA Documents

ADM 1/15745	Donibristle
Air 28/199	Dunino
Air 28/426	Kirknewton
Air 28/459 to 467	Leuchars
Air 29/602	Leuchars
Air 29/684	Grangemouth
Air 29/870	Woodhaven
Air 29/873	Leuchars
Air 29/876	Leuchars
Air 29/1069	Grangemouth
Avia 16/135	Crail

GLOSSARY

ADF — Aircraft Delivery Flight
AFC — Air Force Cross
AOC — Air Officer Commanding
AONS — Air Observer & Navigation School
APC — Armament Practice Camp
BABS Flt — Blind Approach Beam System Flight
BAT Flt — Blind/Beam Approach Training Flight
CANS — Civil Air Navigation School
Capt — Captain
CBE — Commander of the Order of the British Empire
Cdr — Commander
CMG — Companion (of the Order) of St Michael and St George
Comm — Communication
Cpl — Corporal
CTW — Combat Training Wing
Det(s) — Detachment(s)
DFC — Distinguished Flying Cross
DLT — Deck Landing Training
DSC — Distinguished Service Cross
DSO — Distinguished Service Order
E&RFTS — Elementary & Refresher Flying Training School
FAA — Fleet Air Arm
Flg Off — Flying Officer
Flt — Flight
Flt Lt — Flight Lieutenant
Flt Sgt — Flight Sergeant
FTS — Flying Training School
GCB — Knight Grand Cross (of the Order) of the Bath
GCVO — Knight Grand Cross of the Royal Victorian Order
Gp — Group
Gp Capt — Group Captain
GS — Gliding School
HMS — His Majesty's Ship
KCB — Knight Commander of the Order of the Bath
LAC — Leading Aircraftman
Lt — Lieutenant
Lt (A) — Lieutenant (Air Branch)

Lt Cdr — Lieutenant Commander
Lt Cdr(A) — Lieutenant Commander (Air Branch)
Lt Col — Lieutenant Colonel
MAEE — Maritime Aircraft Experimental Establishment
Maj — Major
MC — Military Cross
MT — Motor Transport
MU — Maintenance Unit
OBE — Officer of the Order of the British Empire
Oblt zur See — Lieutenant-seaman officer German Navy
OTU — Operational Training Unit
Plt Off — Pilot Officer
RAAF — Royal Australian Air Force
RCAF — Royal Canadian Air Force
RFC — Royal Flying Corps
RLG — Relief Landing Ground
RM — Royal Marine
RNAS — Royal Naval Air Station
RNethN — Royal Netherlands Navy
RNZAF — Royal New Zealand Air Force
Sgt — Sergeant
SHQ — Station Headquarters
SLG — Satellite Landing Ground
Sqn — Squadron
Sqn Ldr — Squadron Leader
SSQ — Station Sick Quarters
Sub Lt — Sub Lieutenant
Sub Lt (A) — Sub Lieutenant (Air Branch)
TAT — Torpedo Attack Trainer
TBR — Torpedo Bomber Reconnaissance
TDS — Training Depot Squadron
TEU — Tactical Exercise Unit
TRS — Torpedo Refresher Squadron
UAS — University Air Squadron
USAAF — United States Army Air Force
W/O — Warrant Officer
WAAF — Women's Auxiliary Air Force
Wg Cdr — Wing Commander
WRNS — Women's Royal Naval Service
Zerstörer — Destroyer

157

INDEX